THE CORNERSHOP
COOKBOOK

THE CORNERSHOP COOKBOOK

Delicious recipes from your local shop

SOPHIE MISSING & CAROLINE CRAIG

PHOTOGRAPHY BY CHARLOTTE BLAND

■ SQUARE PEG

CONTENTS

INTRODUCTION

The Cornershop Cookbook is a collection of recipes for delicious dishes, made with readily available ingredients from your local cornershop or convenience store. It is a celebration of the fantastic meals you can concoct from the generally ordinary, sometimes untapped, and frequently god-sent ingredients (in that order: hello peanut butter, tinned crab and chorizo) at your disposal locally. From spam to yam, greens to tinned sardines, we've tried it all, and these are the results: a selection of fantastic recipes to suit most evening moods and requirements.

✳

For the majority of people, an amble around a farmers' market remains one of life's luxuries, rather than the norm – something that belongs to the hallowed realms of the weekend, along with sleeping in late, actually reading the papers and making stews that require both a trip to the butcher and a minimum of four hours in the oven. The rest of the time (i.e. the other five days of the week), how we really shop and cook is often a lot less leisurely.

The heyday of the weekly or fortnightly shop, and the trip to a superstore, seems to be over. Many of us have become dependent on the convenience and proximity of the smaller chains and independents that now pepper our routes home. We shop with increasing frequency and haphazardness for food and sundry bits; a spot check of our tote bags might throw up an onion, a pint of milk, ground cumin, E45 cream and the toilet cleaner we've been meaning to replace for weeks. And though we may occasionally push the boat out and do 'a big shop' online (usually after a farcical two hours umming and ahing), our new habitual shops are

largely unplanned, subject to our culinary whims and fancies.

We're not alone, and of course, there's now a phrase for it: top-up shopping. But far from limiting your dinner menu options, given the theoretically smaller range of food on offer, the local shop can open up a world of opportunity and culinary creativity. This book will help you unlock this.

There are ideas and inspiration aplenty out there for getting scrumptious food on the table quickly, slowly, impressively, healthily (our bookshelves bow under the collective weight of these tomes and we bloody adore them!). However, there is the constant issue of how long it actually takes to find and shop for particular ingredients. Often this is completely at odds with the intention of the recipe: to be speedy and effortless – a back pocket no-brainer. Yes, clams take mere moments to cook, look beautiful, and will always impress in an effortlessly delicious spaghetti alle vongole, but are you going to find some in Costcutter?

Probably not. And even if you're lucky enough to live by a butcher or fishmonger, they are generally (and understandably) closed by the time you can get to them after work.

Life doesn't start at the weekend, and don't we deserve some fun, chore-free time and good stuff to eat on a weeknight too? The recipes in this book can be made with ingredients found in local, smaller shops, easily purchased on the way home from work (in fact we almost called this book 'Recipes for the Way Home'). The dishes won't take hours to shop for and assemble, but they will still deliver a delicious end result.

✳

The backbone of the working week, most evenings fall into the category of Chapter One's 'A Quiet Night In'. These are the nights when you need recipes that can be shopped for and put together with little fuss, using largely store cupboard ingredients, and a few additional bits. You won't be cooking for a

crowd, just yourself, and the people you live with, so you can take pleasure from simple yet flavoursome dishes.

On some days though, the thought of another foraged frittata or pesto pasta – or, you know, a spoonful of chutney, followed by two mugs of Alpen – just might not cut the proverbial mustard, and you'll be one step away from dialling the local Thai or Chinese restaurant. This is when we turn to our Chapter Two 'The Alternative Takeaway' recipes, which are as satisfying as ordering in, not to mention cheaper, and quick enough that you won't feel like gnawing your sofa arm off in hunger. You'll wake up the next day light of body and soul, free from the heavy feeling that is the inevitable by-product of eating a dinner that's 98% deep-fried, and without the shame that comes from having spent £2.50 on a bag of greasy prawn crackers that you will probably just throw away.

To quote Nick Hornby quoting Jon Bon Jovi "no man is an island"[1] – and cosy as it is

to stay in scoffing pasta and ploughing through Netflix by yourself, it's nice to have friends round too, sometimes. These don't have to be painstakingly planned or extravagant evenings, as the recipes in Chapter Three, 'The Catch-up Dinner' show: most people are just happy not to have to cook for themselves, and you can serve them DIY sandwiches (AKA the wrap party).

Though we mostly aim to eat fairly healthily, there are evenings when we really fancy something a little bit dirty. You know the score: hot meat in a bun, melted cheese, that kind of thing. The recipes in Chapter Four's 'Dirty Tuesdays' (known as Tequila Tuesdays, by some) celebrate this dark netherworld, in which typical cornershop items (macaroni, frankfurters, instant noodles) really come into their own.

One step up from this type of gathering is Chapter Five's 'The Unplanned Dinner Party'. Also known as the 'oh shit, people are coming round tonight' party. We've all experienced

1 In *About A Boy* (yes, we know it's John Donne, really)

the panic of having to deliver on the Thursday night dinner that seemed like such a good idea when you originally planned it. These recipes – from Mexican themed tacos featuring fish fingers, or a riff on the vegetarian Egyptian dish koshari – will impress without forcing you to a) spend loads, b) run round Tesco like a headless chicken (looking for a chicken), c) be chained to the stove stirring, as everyone else ploughs through the pre-dinner aperitifs.

From a practical perspective, sometimes it's good to plan ahead, and make a little bit more than you need for dinner, so that you can enjoy some for lunch (or indeed, dinner) the next day. Welcome the hearty soups, stews and bakes of Chapter Six's 'Comforting Dinners with Leftover Potential'. This cheering food quietly does its thing on the stove or in the oven while you potter around. Just try not to eat the whole lot in one go.

Finally, no one needs pudding. But sometimes you want it. It's surprising what you can knock together with often overlooked ingredients, as the recipes in Chapter Seven's 'Something Sweet' show – from marshmallow puffed rice and oat cakes, to florentines made from Frosties.

*

'Local shop' is a phrase that encompasses a broad range of places depending on where you live, from an independent family-run cornershop to one of the mini or small branches of the major supermarket chains that – like it or lump it – are an increasingly prominent part of our cities' landscapes. And there is much in between these two extremes: franchised mini chains like Nisa, Costcutter or Londis; a growing number of organic greengrocers and high-end delicatessens; and traditional and not so traditional fruit 'n' veg emporiums, to name but a few. We've outlined some of their strengths and weaknesses.

THE TINY SHOP
(often a newsagent that sells some food)

Generally offering a small range of basics (bread, eggs, milk, tinned stuff, instant noodles) alongside newspapers, and a dazzling array of chocolate.

The good: You can buy a paper or magazine to read while you cook dinner. And – though it hasn't happened to us yet, more's the pity – the EuroMillions ticket you impulse buy while picking up some pitta may be the one.

The annoying: The range of fresh veg can be sparse.

A PROPER CORNERSHOP

So much more than a one-stop-shop for fags and wine. In larger UK cities particularly, they can be an invaluable source of fresh and often exotic fruit and veg: from finger aubergines and bunches of fresh mint and parsley, to plantain, coconuts and durian. And for the growing group who want to shop little and often, access to the constant supply of fresh produce that these stores provide is key.

The good: Obviously this is completely subjective, and depends on where you live, but we find that these shops can have an unequalled selection of 'dry goods'. If you're really lucky, you'll be able to choose between five brands of plum tomatoes, more varieties of beans than you can name, and pasta shapes you've never heard of. The spice section may even rival Ottolenghi's pantry (well, maybe not quite).

The annoying: You're not going to find a pack of high welfare standard king prawns here. The meat fridge can, and often does, contain dubious looking sausages.

THE MINI OR SMALL SUPERMARKET

We don't need to identify these for you. They are everywhere and you can buy pretty

much anything in them, from a shoulder of pork, to home insurance (probably).

The good: Proper meat and fish are strengths and the major things that you won't find at your local. Obviously the quality and variety available is not equal to a fishmonger or butcher, but there are usually a range of cuts at a variety of price points, from organic to free-range, and the basic.

The annoying: Sometimes, inexplicably, you cannot find the strangest things: like a fresh red chilli. They never stock a full range of herbs. And if you want one red pepper, you might have to buy a pack of three, including the green one that no one ever wants and is then stuck with.

✳

Whatever your local shop's pros and cons, we know that right now, when you walk into a small shop, chances are your heart sinks (possibly at the thought of beans on toast and a Dairy Milk chaser). But you needn't worry: this book will open your eyes to of the untapped potential at your fingertips and inspire you to make something delicious. These recipes are all about enjoying something good to eat, without spending those precious post-work hours battling in a supermarket aisle, or in front of the stove. Some may be twists on the familiar, some may be something new – but we hope that many will make their way into your regular dinner repertoire.

We hope that this will be the book you turn to on your way home, when you haven't a clue what to make with what's available, and when you need inspiration to whip up another dinner from everyday, yet sometimes overlooked, ingredients. More than anything, our aim is to show you that though the product range of your local shop(s) may be limited, your meal options don't have to be.

A NOTE ON QUANTITIES

Our chapters are organised by how you might eat and cook of an evening. So, while there are many recipes for one or two, these are always written so that they can be easily doubled, tripled or quadrupled, if necessary.

SUBSTITUTING INGREDIENTS

Naturally, we cannot account for the range in every single local shop in the country, and there may well be some ingredients that you are unable to get, on a particular night, for a particular recipe, in your particular shop. Maybe it's a bunch of kale. Or something as unassuming as a lime. Whatever it may be, we have tried to allow for this in the book where possible, offering suggestions for ingredient alternatives, swaps and recipe permutations to help. Overall though, what we are trying to convey is that we should all have the confidence to just use what we have

easy access to, swapping fresh for tinned, dried or pickled where necessary, because frankly, life is too short to worry about not having all the exact ingredients for a dish.

If you have your own ideas for replacement ingredients that might work well, by all means go with them! Having to replace ingredients forces you to develop your culinary creativity: sometimes the resulting meal will become a firm favourite, other times it might be rather less successful – but at least you tried.

The Basics +
How to Shop for Them

By 'basic' we mean that most (stress on most) of these items should be available from your local shop, so that if you do unexpectedly run out, you can easily replace them. This list is, obviously, personal — one person's peanut butter is another's Marmite — as is the suggested timeline for replacing items. If you're a heavy pasta consumer, then you may well need to replace it more often than every couple of months.

Top Up Once a Week

Tinned

Beans and pulses: borlotti/butter/cannellini/
   red kidney beans, chickpeas
Fish: anchovies in oil (tinned or jarred),
   mackerel, sardines, tuna, crab
Tomatoes: whole plum or chopped

Fresh

Bread: regular and a stash of pitta for
   (bread-based) emergencies (freeze any
   leftovers for toasting)
Cheese: Cheddar, feta, Parmesan
Chillies
Eggs (we use medium)
Fruit and vegetables: an assortment,
   depending on what you like and use most
   (e.g. aubergines, cabbage, carrots, lettuce,
   potatoes, tomatoes)
Lemons
Limes
Onions: white and at least one red
Yoghurt: natural (like Total
   Greek-style yoghurt)

Top Up Fortnightly

Fresh

Chorizo (we use a chorizo ring, usually sold
   in a 225g packet)
Garlic
Ginger
Herbs: such as basil, chives, coriander,
   mint, parsley, rosemary, thyme. Remove
   from the packaging and wrap in a damp
   tea towel in the fridge to prolong
   their life — or grow your own (see
   overleaf)
Bacon

Top Up Once a Month or So

Fridge
Butter: unsalted

Packets
Ready-to-bake baguettes

Top Up Every Few Months or as Necessary

Jarred
Capers
Mustard: Colman's/English, Dijon
Peanut butter: crunchy and smooth
Pickles: beetroot, gherkins or cornichons,
  onions
Tomato purée

Packets
Pasta: we tend to hoard a range of different
  dried pastas, but would recommend one
  long shape like spaghetti or linguine, and
  one tubular type, like penne or macaroni.
  Wholewheat pasta is increasingly readily
  available and good for variety too.
Rice: brown and white — basmati, long-grain

Bottles
Chilli oil (see recipe for DIY Garlic Chilli Oil
  on page 61)
Oil: a neutral vegetable oil for cooking (such
  as groundnut oil), olive oil, extra-virgin
  olive oil
Soy sauce
Tomato ketchup
Vinegar: red wine, white wine

Freezer
Bread (as before)
Peas

Spice and herb drawer
Bay leaves
Black peppercorns
Cayenne pepper
Chilli flakes

Cinnamon: ground and sticks
Coriander: whole seeds and ground
Cumin: whole seeds and ground
Curry powder
Nutmeg: whole
Sea salt (such as Maldon) and table salt (we
  always use sea salt, unless salting water for
  pasta or similar)
Smoked paprika

Cupboard
Bouillon powder, and chicken, beef, fish and
  vegetable individual jelly stock pots or
  stock cubes
Golden syrup
Honey
Marmite
Plain flour
Sugar: caster, granulated, icing,
  soft light brown

Grow

Basil
Mint
Rosemary
Thyme

The Slightly Less Basic but Really Good to Have

You may think that this should be filed under 'bleeding obvious', but opportunities to stock up on more difficult to find items should be seized as and when they present themselves (when you're used to shopping for one evening at a time, it can be easy to forget about looking further ahead).

Chilli sauce: sriracha, sweet chilli sauce
Fish sauce
Noodles: dried, ready-to-cook, instant/
 straight-to-wok; egg, rice, ramen, wheat
 flour — whatever you can find
Pine nuts
Rice wine vinegar
Sesame oil
Star anise
Sumac

A QUIET NIGHT IN

If we were to ask people to be completely honest about what they cook for themselves, on a night in, alone, some of their replies would be weird and wonderful. And probably completely unpublishable (gherkin pasta, anyone?). We concoct strange, sometimes decadent, sometimes disastrous, things when we are by ourselves, impatient and hungry. There's no one there to pass judgement on our unconventional creations, and no one to impress. For many of us then, free from these (often imaginary) restrictions, these are the times when we truly make do with what we have, combined with what we may have picked up excitedly from the local shop on the way home.

But this chapter isn't really about 'wacky' cooking for one (though we may stray into that later). It's about being honest about the flavoursome, yet simple dishes we are most likely to crave and enjoy making on a quiet night in, and having the confidence to make a meal out of not too much. It's about convenience, comfort, and not making your evening more chore-filled than it has to be – and that includes minimising the washing up (especially if you don't have a dishwasher). These recipes aren't about spending ages in the kitchen, or dashing madly around the shop on your way home, trying to locate an essential packet of Thai basil leaves (or, you know, whatever the thing is that you need to buy that is inevitably out of stock). They are the ones we turn to on most low-key weeknights (or weekends), especially in autumn or winter, when the siren call of a balmy alfresco drink or post-work activity is pretty much non existent, and the desire to hibernate and eat bowls of good things in front of Netflix is strong.

Unsurprisingly, pasta – probably the most popular convenience food of our time – is a dominant theme, paired with speedy sauces that pack a punch. (Without gherkins though, you'll be pleased to hear.)

Linguine with Tinned Crab

If there's anything better in life than a large, steaming bowl of pasta, then we haven't yet found it. This recipe is for one, but the quantities can easily be upped if you want to make this for more people.

You can buy handpicked crabmeat in some fancier local shops (hello, mini Waitrose), but you can find either tinned white crabmeat chunks or brown 'dressed' crabmeat in most local shops, nestled next to the tinned tuna and sardines. It tastes surprisingly good and is perfect in this pasta, where the delicate flavour of fresh crab might be lost alongside the chilli and garlic.

Serves 1

Preparation time: 5 minutes
Cooking time: 10 minutes

2 tbsp olive oil
1 garlic clove, thinly sliced
½ red chilli, seeded and chopped (use dried if you can't find a fresh one)

1 x 43g tin 'dressed' crabmeat or ⅓ x 170g tin white crabmeat chunks (drained)
90g linguine
finely grated zest and juice of ½ lemon
salt and freshly ground black pepper

Put a pan of salted water on to boil for the pasta. Add the oil to a separate pan and fry the garlic for a couple of minutes (don't let it colour), then add the chilli and cook for another minute before adding the crabmeat. Add your pasta to the pan of boiling water and, while it's cooking, zest the lemon. Once al dente, drain the pasta and combine immediately with the crab mix. Stir in the lemon zest, then squeeze over the lemon juice. Enjoy immediately, seasoning to taste.

Venetian Spaghetti

Onion and anchovy might sound like an odd and even unappealing basis for a sauce, but slow cooking (and butter) transform them into a rich, savoury sauce – much more than the sum of their parts. This is the sort of pasta dinner that you can probably make with the stuff you already have in the cupboard, or shop for with the scrabbled together change found down the back of the sofa.

People often say you should only cook with a wine you'd be happy to drink. Interpret this advice as best you can when faced with your local shop's selection of vintage Lambrini.

Serves 2

Preparation time: 5 minutes (depending on how quickly you chop your onions)
Cooking time: 30 minutes

2 tbsp extra-virgin olive oil
10g butter
2 large onions

8 anchovies
125ml white wine or water
125ml milk
180g wholewheat spaghetti or pasta of your choice
salt and freshly ground black pepper

Add the oil and butter to a saucepan and put on a low-ish heat. Halve and thinly slice the onions, and once the butter has melted, add to the pan. Cook for 5 minutes, until the onions start to turn a bit golden – make sure they don't go too brown though. At this point, add the anchovies and a splash of the wine or water. Leave to cook for another 20 minutes, adding the remainder of the wine or water, then the milk, every time the onion mix looks like it is beginning to dry out.

When the sauce is nearing readiness, put a separate saucepan of salted water on to boil. Cook the spaghetti for just under the amount of time specified on the packet, then drain well (reserving some of the cooking water) and add it to the onion-anchovy sauce. Give it all a good mix together and add a splash of the pasta cooking water if you think it needs a bit more sauciness. Cook for another minute, then season liberally with lots of black pepper before serving.

Panzanella

A Tuscan salad made from ingredients that are readily available in even the tiniest of cornershops. The danger here is the tomatoes: there are few things worse than rock hard, flavourless tomatoes, so if you can't find ripe ones, then use cherry or baby plum tomatoes instead and roast them very briefly with a sprinkling of olive oil to encourage them to become juicy and sweet. As with most of these recipes for 1, scale up as necessary. If you can't find nice bread, you could use pitta for a panzanella-fattoush hybrid.

Serves 1

Preparation time: 20 minutes
Cooking time: 10 minutes

1½ tbsp olive oil
2 anchovies (optional)
1 garlic clove, crushed
1 tbsp red wine vinegar

3 thick-ish slices of stale bread
1 red pepper
2 tomatoes, cored and roughly chopped,
    or 10–12 cherry or baby plum tomatoes,
    quartered
1 tbsp capers
salt and freshly ground black pepper

First things first: preheat your oven grill or grill to high.

Add the oil to the bowl that you are planning to serve the salad in. Add the anchovies, if using, to the oil and smoosh with the back of a tablespoon so they break down. Add the garlic and red wine vinegar and taste, adding more oil or vinegar as necessary.

Toast the bread on both sides and then chop or rip into bits.

Place the red pepper on a baking tray and grill, turning every few minutes, until the pepper skin is black and blistered. Once it has reached this state, remove and leave until cool enough to handle. (If your tomatoes are a bit sad and un-juicy, now is the time to help them along by giving them 10 minutes in the oven.)

Peel the skin off the pepper and, discarding the seeds and core, rip into long shreds. Take care not to lose all the good pepper juice. Add the pepper shreds and the tomatoes and their juice to the salad bowl and mix together, then add the capers, mix again and add seasoning to taste. Add the toasted bread pieces and mix together again, then serve.

Sort of Puttanesca

Puttanesca is one of our all-time favourite things to eat, partly because it is the ultimate store cupboard saviour supper, and partly because it's just really delicious. This recipe is a sunny alternative to the traditional tinned tomato-based sauce – lighter, but with all the same strong flavours. If you have a red or yellow pepper knocking around your fridge drawer, by all means thinly slice it and roast along with the tomatoes.

Serves 2

Preparation time: 5 minutes
Cooking time: around 20 minutes

350g cherry or baby plum tomatoes
2 garlic cloves
2 tbsp olive oil, plus extra for serving
½ tsp dried chilli flakes

180g pasta of your choice – linguine or
    spaghetti work well
4 anchovies
1 heaped tbsp small capers (chop them
    roughly if they are large)
salt and freshly ground black pepper

Preheat the oven to 200°C/gas 6.

Halve the tomatoes and add to a small ovenproof dish. Crush the garlic and add with the oil, chilli flakes and salt and pepper and give the dish a good shake so that everything mixes together. Roast for 10 minutes.

Fill a decent-sized pan with salted water and bring to the boil before adding the pasta. Remove the tomatoes from the oven, add the anchovies, giving the dish a further shake, and roast for another 10 minutes, or until the pasta is ready.

Drain the pasta well, reserving a small mugful of the starchy water. Add the capers to the tomatoes and anchovies and mix well. The anchovies should have broken down into the tomato juice, producing a thin sauce. Add the pasta and mix together. If you need to add a little of the reserved pasta water, do so now. Season with more salt, pepper and oil before serving.

Slaw with Shredded Star Anise Chicken

Cheap, delicious, fragrant and healthy, this slaw has become a go-to weeknight dish for us since our friend J made a version for Caroline. It can be made with any combination of vegetables you wish: carrot, fennel, white cabbage, red cabbage, etc. Try not to compromise on the fresh herbs we suggest as they really lift it; use one at the very least.

Serves 4

Preparation time: 10 minutes
Cooking time: 25 minutes

For the shredded star anise chicken
4 skinless, boneless chicken breasts
2 cinnamon sticks, snapped in half
4 garlic cloves, skin on but quickly bashed
4 star anise
thumb-sized piece of ginger, peeled
1 tbsp sesame oil
salt and freshly ground black pepper

For the dressing
3 tbsp sesame oil
2 tsp rice wine vinegar
1 tsp fish sauce
1 tsp honey
juice of ½ lime

1 garlic clove, crushed
1cm piece of ginger, peeled and grated

For the slaw
1 red onion
1kg any combination of the following: white
   cabbage, red cabbage, radishes, celery,
   carrots, young turnips, kohlrabi
20g fresh coriander, leaves picked
20g fresh mint, leaves picked
20g fresh parsley, leaves picked
sprinkling of seeds, such as sesame and
   pumpkin seeds

mayonnaise, to serve (optional)

To make the chicken, preheat the oven to 180°C/gas 4. Line a baking tray with foil, ensuring that you have enough slack at the sides to join at the top to form a parcel.

Pop the chicken breasts in the foil, and top each with half a cinnamon stick, a garlic clove and a star anise. Grate over the ginger, grind over some black pepper, then finish with a drizzle of sesame oil. Close the foil over the top to form a parcel. Bake for 20–25 minutes, until the breasts are cooked through.

While the chicken is cooking, prepare your dressing and slaw. Start by taking a large salad bowl or serving dish and adding all the dressing ingredients: use a fork to give everything a whisk, adding seasoning to taste.

Now attend to your vegetables for the slaw. Many Chinese supermarkets sell a rather nifty julienning peeler which comes in handy at this stage. Thinly slice your red onion, cabbages, radishes and celery. Peel and julienne any large root veg (carrots, turnips, kohlrabi) if using – you could also use a vegetable peeler to make them into ribbons.

Roughly chop the herbs and add almost all to the serving dish, setting some aside for the topping. Now, even though the chicken probably isn't quite ready yet, we like to dress the salad at this stage as it ever so slightly softens the crunchy veg, so add all the veg to the dressing and give that slaw a good mix.

When the chicken breasts are cooked, discard the cinnamon, garlic and star anise and chop or shred the chicken into chunks. Sprinkle over some salt to taste and add the lot to the slaw, mixing well. Top with the remaining herbs and the seeds, and serve with mayonnaise on the side, if you like.

PEELING GINGER

The best and least wasteful tip we've been given on how to peel ginger is to use a teaspoon to scrape the skin off.

Herby Vegetable Gratin

There are times when you just want to get something warm and flavoursome in the oven without much hassle. This simple gratin sends lovely herby aromas throughout your house.

Serves 4

Preparation time: 10 minutes
Cooking time: 1 hour 10 minutes

4 tbsp extra-virgin olive oil
2 courgettes
500g small-ish potatoes
6 tomatoes

20g basil leaves
generous splash of white wine
squeeze of lemon juice (about ¼ lemon)
1 tsp dried thyme
150ml hot vegetable stock
75g feta cheese
salt and freshly ground black pepper

Preheat the oven to 200°C/gas 6 and lightly oil the bottom of a large gratin dish using 1 tablespoon of the oil.

Wash the vegetables, leaving the skin on, then slice, thinly (about 2mm thick). Roll up a tea towel and place it under one end of the dish to raise it slightly, so it will make filling the dish easier. Starting at the lowered end of the dish, pack the slices upright (vertically), alternating courgette, potato and tomato slices and basil leaves, in rows or in a snail pattern depending on the shape of your dish or your artistic inclination. Any leftover slices can be tucked in here and there.

Season with salt and pepper, then sprinkle over the wine, lemon juice and thyme. Drizzle over the remaining oil.

Bake for about 40 minutes, then take out, pour over the stock and crumble over the feta. Return to the oven for a further 30 minutes, or until the potatoes are cooked and the top is nice and crispy in parts.

Pesto Pasta with Oven-Dried Tomatoes and Feta

This simple supper calls for red pesto and some oven-dried cherry tomatoes: a process which intensifies their flavour and along with the cinnamon, gives them a tasty kick. Making your own pesto can be easy with the help of a blender and copious amounts of fresh herbs, but there's nothing like the convenience of a jar. Smaller independent shops can stock little known delectable Italian brands. So cheat away.

Serves 4

Preparation time: 5 minutes
Cooking time: 1 hour

200g cherry tomatoes
extra-virgin olive oil, for drizzling
pinch or two of ground cinnamon

500g wholewheat spaghetti
1 x 190g jar red pesto
salt and freshly ground black pepper
feta cheese, to serve
basil leaves, to finish

Just over an hour before you are due to eat, preheat the oven to a nice low temperature, around 140°C/gas 1.

Slice the cherry tomatoes in half along their equator and lay, cut sides facing up, on a baking tray. Drizzle a drop or two of oil on each tomato, followed by a little sprinkling of cinnamon and salt and pepper. Pop in the oven and leave to slowly, slowly cook for an hour.

About 15 minutes before you are ready to serve, put a large pan of salted water on to boil and cook the spaghetti until al dente. Drain the pasta and add the pesto, mixing well.

Dish out the spaghetti and top each portion with crumbled feta, the now oven-dried and intensely flavoured tomatoes, and a few snips of basil. Serve with a green salad, and some lovely red wine.

Sardine Pasta with Lemon Breadcrumbs

This is an entry-level tinned sardine recipe, with lots of strong flavours standing up to the fish. We think the slightly rougher texture of wholewheat pasta goes well with the sauce, but really, use whatever you have to hand. If you can't find cavolo nero or other green cabbage, you could use broccoli, finely chopped.

Serves 2

Preparation time: 5 minutes
Cooking time: 30 minutes

1½ slices of bread, the staler the better (you could also use pitta)
4½ tbsp extra-virgin olive oil
finely grated zest of 1 lemon
2 garlic cloves, thinly sliced
½ tsp dried chilli flakes
150g cavolo nero or other green cabbage, chopped (or use pre-chopped)
1 x 120g tin sardines in oil
180g wholewheat fusilli or other smallish pasta like penne
salt and freshly ground black pepper

Rip the bread up roughly and blitz into rough breadcrumbs in a small food processor or with a hand-held blender. If you don't have a food processor, chop with a sharp knife until a small crumb-like consistency is reached.

Add 2 tablespoons of the oil to a pan and leave to heat for a couple of minutes. Add the breadcrumbs and fry on a medium heat for around 7 minutes or until crisp. Season with salt and half of the lemon zest. When done, scrape out into a bowl.

Heat the remaining oil in a sauté pan and add the garlic. Cook gently for a minute (don't let it colour!), before adding the chilli flakes and cabbage. Cook with the lid on for 5 minutes.

Drain off most of the sardine oil – and if there are large bones or bits of skin, remove them – then add the fillets to the sauté pan, with a little of the sardine oil. Season and cook on a low heat, with the lid on, for 10 minutes.

While this is cooking, put a large pan of salted water on to boil for the pasta. When it's bubbling away, add the pasta and cook for 2 minutes under the recommended time given on the packet.

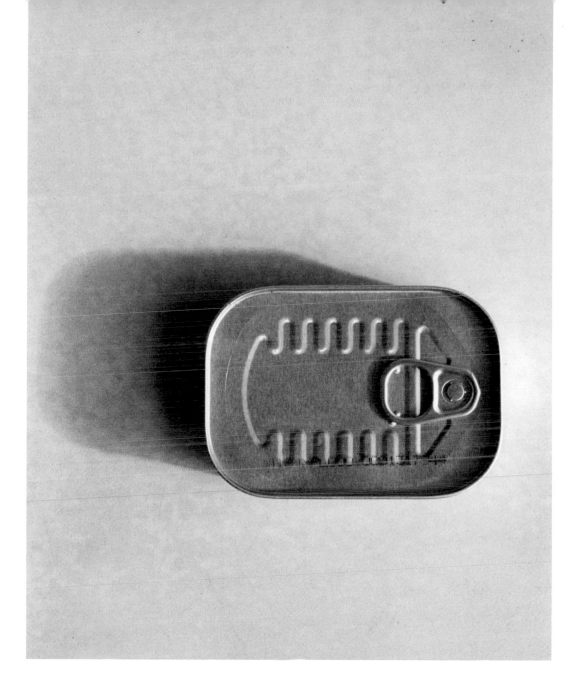

Drain the pasta, reserving some of its cooking water, then add the pasta to the sardine and cabbage mix, stirring so that it is coated well. Add a splash of the reserved cooking water and the rest of the lemon zest, and cook for a couple of minutes on a low heat, adding more cooking water if necessary (the water helps create a sort of sauce, coating the pasta).

Serve the breadcrumbs on the side to sprinkle on top of the pasta.

Fritters, Four Ways

Beetroot, Carrot and Feta Fritters

Fried things are generally delicious, and these fritters, with their hint of cheese, are no exception. Make sure the mixture is firm enough to hold together, that the oil is hot and that you don't move the fritters until they've formed a bit of a crust. A spatula is handy here; a chopstick, less so. Serve with garlic yoghurt and a green salad with a mustardy dressing for a light-ish dinner. Using gram flour makes these gluten free, but you can use plain flour too.

Makes 8 fritters/Serves 4

Preparation time: 15 minutes
Cooking time: 25 minutes

For the fritters
1 large raw beetroot, scrubbed (or use
    a packet of ready-cooked beets) — total
    weight 250g
1 large carrot, scrubbed
6 spring onions
1 tsp ground cumin
1 x 400g tin chickpeas, drained and rinsed
1 egg, beaten

4 tbsp gram flour or plain flour (plus a little
    extra, if needed)
150g feta cheese
salt and freshly ground black pepper
vegetable oil, for frying

For the garlic yoghurt
1 garlic clove, peeled
good pinch of salt
6 tbsp natural yoghurt

Start by making the fritters. Coarsely grate the beetroot and carrot into a large bowl. Finely chop the spring onions (including the green ends) and add to the veg, then add the cumin, along with a good pinch of salt and some pepper. Add the chickpeas, crushing them with your hands as you pour them into the bowl. Mix together until everything is well combined. Add the egg, then the gram flour and mix well. If the mixture seems too wet to handle, add a bit more flour. Finally, crumble in the feta, and give it all a good mix.

Add enough oil to cover the bottom of a frying pan and heat until very hot (you can throw in a little piece of the veg mix to test it; if it sizzles then you're good to go). Scoop a heaped tablespoon of the mixture from the bowl, form it into a round patty in your hands and place in the pan. Repeat twice.

Leave the patties to cook for 30 seconds, before pressing down on them with a spatula, so they squish out and become larger and thinner. Fry for around 4 minutes on each side, until crisp and golden. Remove to a plate lined with kitchen towel and keep warm while you cook the remaining fritters in batches (3 in the pan at a time works best for us).

For the garlic yoghurt, make a garlic-salt paste (a pestle and mortar is easiest for this, we find), then mix in the yoghurt. Serve alongside the fritters.

Fennel, Red Onion and Parmesan Fritters

A green salad alongside a fritter is no bad thing.

Makes 8 fritters/Serves 4

Preparation time: 15 minutes
Cooking time: 25 minutes

2 fennel bulbs
1 small red onion
40g Parmesan or other hard cheese
1 x 400g tin chickpeas, drained and rinsed

1 egg, beaten
4 tbsp gram flour or plain flour (plus a little
  extra, if needed)
salt and freshly ground black pepper
vegetable oil, for frying

Trim the fennel bulbs, cut the hard bottom section out, and slice as finely as possible using a mandoline or your sharpest knife – as though you're chopping an onion. Slice the red onion to a similar size. Roughly chop all the veg so there aren't any large bits. Transfer to a bowl and season with salt (be a bit sparing as the cheese will be salty) and pepper, then grate in the Parmesan using a coarse grater. Add the chickpeas, crushing them with your hands as you pour them into the bowl. Mix together until everything is well combined. Add the egg, then the gram flour and mix well. If the mixture seems too wet to handle, add a bit more flour.

Add enough oil to cover the bottom of the pan and heat until very hot (you can throw in a little piece of the veg mix to test it if you want; if it sizzles then you're good to go). Scoop a heaped tablespoon of the fritter mixture from the bowl, form it into a ball-shaped patty in your hands and place in the pan. Repeat twice more.

Leave the patties to cook for 30 seconds, before pressing down on them with a spatula, so they squish out and become larger and thinner. Fry for around 4 minutes on each side, until crisp and golden. Remove to a plate lined with kitchen towel and keep warm, while you cook the remaining fritters in batches (3 in the pan at a time works best for us). Serve with a green salad.

Courgette, Cannellini and Lemon Fritters

A delightfully zesty fritter. This makes a damper mix than the previous two recipes (which is why it calls for slightly more flour) so, rather than shaping the patties with your hands, dollop the veg batter directly into the pan.

Makes 8 fritters/Serves 4

Preparation time: 15 minutes
Cooking time: 25–30 minutes

2 courgettes (around 450g)
1 x 400g tin cannellini beans, drained
   and rinsed
50g Cheddar
1 egg, beaten

6 tbsp gram flour or plain flour (plus a little
   extra, if needed)
zest of 1 large lemon
½ tsp dried chilli flakes
salt and freshly ground black pepper
vegetable oil, for frying

Coarsely grate the courgettes into a large bowl. Decant into a sieve and squeeze out as much liquid as possible before returning to the bowl. Season with salt (be a bit sparing as the cheese will be salty) and pepper. Add the cannellini beans, crushing them slightly with your hands as you pour them into the bowl. Mix together until everything is well combined. Grate in the Cheddar, then add the egg, then the gram flour, lemon zest and chilli flakes and mix well. If the mixture seems too wet to handle, add a bit more flour.

Add enough oil to cover the bottom of a frying pan and heat until very hot (you can throw in a little piece of the veg mix to test it if you want; if it sizzles then you're good to go). Scoop a heaped tablespoon of the fritter mixture from the bowl and carefully place in the pan. Repeat twice more.

Leave the patties to cook for 30 seconds, before pressing down on them with a spatula, so they squish out and become larger and thinner. Fry for around 4 minutes on each side, until crisp and golden. Remove to a plate lined with kitchen towel and keep warm, while you cook the remaining fritters in batches (3 in the pan at a time works best for us). Serve with a green salad.

Tinned Crab and Corn Cakes

A meal from predominantly tinned ingredients that does not involve cracking into a Fray Bentos (not that we are averse...). Whenever we see tinned crabmeat we pounce on it and make these cakes or our linguine (see page 24). Delicious with sweet potato wedges, or a salad for a lighter combo.

Makes 4/Serves 2

Preparation time: 10 minutes
Cooking time: 10 minutes

1 x 170g tin crabmeat (120g drained weight)
1 x 198g tin sweetcorn (80g drained weight)
4 spring onions
½ red chilli

2 eggs, beaten
50g breadcrumbs
squeeze or dash of chilli sauce (like Sriracha or Tabasco)
salt and freshly ground black pepper
3 tbsp vegetable oil

Drain the crab and sweetcorn and add to a large bowl.

Finely slice the spring onions and seed and chop the chilli. Add to the bowl along with the eggs. Mix together thoroughly, then add the breadcrumbs, chilli sauce and salt and pepper. Mix again.

Form into 4 equal sized patties (around 90g each) – be careful as they'll be fairly delicate creatures to handle.

Next, heat the oil in a large frying pan. When hot enough to sizzle (but not smoking), add the cakes.

Cook for 4 minutes on each side on a medium to high heat, taking care that they don't burn. Serve immediately with some sweet chilli sauce.

Roman Spaghetti

So called as it's our version of that Roman classic, Amatriciana. The inclusion of onions is a controversial subject but we are firmly pro. We use pancetta or bacon in place of the traditional guanciale (not your everyday cornershop ingredient, sadly) and Parmesan can be substituted for pecorino. Perfect for whipping up after a few post work drinks when you need something filling and delicious, stat. It arguably tastes even better the next day.

Can only find smoked bacon? Not a problem. If you're worried about it being too overpowering, blanch it in boiling water for a minute before patting dry, snipping and frying as directed.

Serves 3 — 4

Preparation time: 10 minutes
Cooking time: 25 minutes

1 large red onion
2 tbsp olive oil
6 rashers pancetta or unsmoked streaky
   or regular bacon
½ tsp dried chilli flakes

1 tbsp tomato purée
1 x 500g carton or jar passata
360g spaghetti — bucatini is the ideal
   but spaghetti or linguine are
   admirable substitutes
salt and freshly ground black pepper
grated pecorino or Parmesan, to serve

Put a large pot of salted water on to boil. Halve the onion, then slice into thin-ish half moons.

Add the oil to a large, deep saucepan on a medium heat and after a minute, add the onion slices. Cook until they have just gone past the soft stage, then add the pancetta or bacon – instead of chopping, we use scissors to cut it into small pieces over the pan. Continue cooking until it starts to crisp – pancetta will reach this stage far more quickly than bacon. Add the chilli flakes and cook for a couple of minutes – until they start to colour the oil red – then add the tomato purée and cook for a couple of minutes more. Pour in the passata. Rinse the carton or jar out with water and add this to the pan too so you don't waste anything. Taste and season with salt and pepper, if necessary (depending on saltiness imparted by your bacon), then cook on a relatively high heat for 10 minutes.

By now the water should be boiling. Add the spaghetti and cook for just under the time specified on the packet. While it cooks, leave your sauce on a medium heat until it has thickened and reduced a little. When you come to drain the spaghetti, reserve half a mugful of the cooking water. Add the spaghetti to the tomato-pancetta sauce, combine, and then add a splash of the cooking water if it needs loosening. Cook for a minute, season with lots of black pepper and serve with grated pecorino or Parmesan

Can't find bacon at all? Use half a 200g tin of spam (see page 132 for how to use remainder) chopped into lardon-like pieces. Just call it Spamatriciana.

Egg Hash with Guacamole

There are some evenings when the moment you step in through the front door you make a beeline for your fridge: time is of the essence and if you don't have a quick dinner on the go sharpish you will find yourself eating pesto from the jar. Egg hash is the ideal choice in this scenario as it is quick to prepare. We serve it alongside guacamole as it is a wholesome, flavoursome tummy pleaser and also very much a friend of the egg. Chilli sauce and plenty of buttered toast are welcome additions.

Serves 2 — 3

Preparation time: 8 minutes
Cooking time: 8 minutes

For the guacamole
2 ripe avocados
½ red chilli
½ red onion
handful of cherry tomatoes
20g fresh coriander
juice of 2 limes (about 3 tbsp)
salt and freshly ground black pepper

For the egg hash
1 tbsp olive oil
1 onion
1 red pepper
coriander stalks (reserved from above)
½ tsp smoked paprika
½ tsp cayenne pepper
6 eggs

Start with the guacamole. Slice the avocados in half and remove the stones. Scoop out the flesh and place in a bowl, then mash as best you can using a fork. Seed and finely chop the chilli, finely chop the onion and quarter the cherry tomatoes. Add to the bowl. Remove the coriander stalks (reserve them for the egg hash) and roughly chop the leaves before adding to the avocado mix. Sprinkle over plenty of salt and the lime juice, then mix and taste to check the seasoning. Set aside.

Now, attend to your egg hash. Put the oil in a large frying pan on a medium heat. Thinly slice the onion and add to the pan. Cook for a few minutes while you seed and roughly chop the red pepper and thinly slice the reserved coriander stalks. Add both to the pan and continue cooking for a further 3–4 minutes until the onion is soft and translucent, then sprinkle over the spices. While the onion and pepper finish cooking, crack the eggs into a bowl and whisk, adding salt and pepper. Pour into the pan, a minute after you've added the spices, and using a wooden spoon, stir continuously to cook evenly.

Serve immediately with the guacamole, plenty of buttered bread or toast and a dash or two of chilli sauce.

Potato and Green Bean Garlic Salad

Whether or not this qualifies as a salad is a contentious issue, but our general policy of 'if there's a dressing on it, then it most probably is' has overruled the crowd in this instance.

Very much more than the sum of its parts, the warm potatoes and green beans are brought to life with a garlicky French dressing. We keep the dressing ingredients on the table after dishing out, garlic and garlic press included, as people inevitably go back for more when they realise what a marriage made in heaven this is.

Serves 4

Preparation time: 10 minutes
Cooking time: 20 minutes

800g potatoes (any buttery, salad variety will do)
500g green beans

For the dressing
4 garlic cloves, crushed
8 tbsp good-quality extra-virgin olive oil
2 tbsp good-quality red wine vinegar
salt and freshly ground black pepper

Wash the potatoes, peeling if you wish, and chop to a uniform size if some are on the large side. Decant into the largest pan you own and cover with cold water. Add salt and place on a medium to high heat on the hob. Bring to the boil, then lower the heat a little and cook for 10 minutes.

Top and tail the green beans, if untrimmed, and after the potatoes have cooked for 10 minutes, add the green beans to the same pan, topping up with extra boiling water from the kettle, if necessary. Cook together for a final 4–5 minutes, then check that the potatoes are nice and soft by using a knife to pierce one. If ready, drain the lot and then place back in the pan, mixing slightly to evenly spread out the beans and potatoes for ease of serving. Leave to sit, lid off for a few minutes, while you prepare the dressing.

People can be particular about how garlicky they like their food so you could simply leave all the ingredients on the table and let your guests make their own dressing, leading by example with a bold whole clove crushed on your serving… It is, however, much easier to make one big batch of dressing as per the quantities here (just whisk all the ingredients together in a small bowl) and spoon it over the potatoes and beans in the big pan, before tossing and dishing out.

Tuna Polpette

More fishball, than meatball, really. To avoid dryness, make them small (teaspoon size) rather than hefty, and be sure to add the lemon zest.

This recipe makes 9–10 small polpette. Enjoy as a snack (stick in a few cocktail sticks and pretend you're in Italy) or with a simple tomato sauce and pasta to make it a proper meal.

Serves 2

Preparation time: 10 minutes
Cooking time: 25 minutes

3 tbsp vegetable, groundnut or
    sunflower oil, for frying

For the polpette
1 x 160g tin tuna (in oil or water)
1 tsp finely grated lemon zest
¼ tsp dried chilli flakes
2 tbsp dried breadcrumbs
1 egg
small handful of chopped fresh parsley
    (optional)
salt and freshly ground black pepper

For the tomato and pasta sauce
1 garlic clove
1 tbsp olive oil
pinch of dried chilli flakes
1 x 400g carton or jar tomato passata
180g pasta of your choice

For the polpette, drain the tuna, and give it a good squeeze to get rid of any excess oil or water. In a mixing bowl, combine it with the lemon zest, chilli flakes, a good grinding of black pepper, a pinch of salt and the breadcrumbs. Crack in the egg and mix together until well combined (add the parsley too, if you have any). Mould teaspoonfuls of the mixture into little balls – this amount should make around 9 or 10 – and place on a plate.

To make the tomato sauce, crush the garlic, add the olive oil to a saucepan and cook the garlic for a minute on a low heat, until softened. Add the chilli flakes, and leave to infuse the oil for a minute or two, then add the tomato passata. Cook on a medium heat for 15–20 minutes – you want it to reduce down a bit, and become glossy. Season to taste.

While the sauce cooks, put on a pot of salted water for the pasta. When it's boiling, cook the pasta until al dente, then drain.

While the pasta is cooking, fry the polpette. Heat the vegetable oil in a frying pan on a fairly high heat until it's sizzling but not burning hot. Add your little balls and fry for around 7 minutes, giving them a delicate shuffle every now and then so that they get evenly brown and crisp.

If serving with sauce, add the balls to the pan of tomato sauce and coat, then mix in the cooked and drained pasta when ready.

THE ALTERNATIVE TAKEAWAY

Generally there's nothing we enjoy more than coming home, switching on the radio, pouring a stiff drink and making something good to eat from whatever weird scraps are knocking around, plus whatever we've picked up on the way.

But sometimes – after an especially tiring day, if we're feeling uninspired, or if we just really fancy a steaming hot pho, or taste bud-awakening curry, say – it can be difficult to resist the siren call of the takeaway, especially now that you can order pretty much anything you want online in a couple of clicks, without the double inconvenience of having to speak to an actual human or running to the cashpoint.

While there is absolutely, 100%, a time and a place for a takeaway, all too often it's just a convenient crutch to fall back on. And what we have found is that, laziness aside, what we're generally really after from takeaways is strong, savoury flavours and a tingly mouth.

So stay stalwart: we've put together a chapter that is homage to all that is garlicky, spicy and more-ish – without the expense of a takeaway or the caloric consequence.

Spicy Asian-Style Turkey and Greens Soup

This restorative soup is a perfect speedy midweek supper – just the thing for a gloomy evening.

Turkey mince is ideal here because of its leanness, and it is – oddly – often easier to find than pork in convenience stores (though not that mainstay of spag bol, chilli con carne, cottage pie et al, beef mince). If you can't get hold of any though, you could substitute 2 chicken breasts, poached with a clove of bashed garlic, some peppercorns and a stub of ginger. Shred it before adding to the pan with the chilli flakes and black pepper.

Serves 2 generously

Preparation time: 10 minutes
**Cooking time: around 15 minutes (add
    an extra 20 minutes poaching time if
    substituting chicken breasts)**

2 garlic cloves
2.5cm piece of ginger, peeled
200g turkey mince
2 tsp groundnut oil
1 chicken stock cube or individual
    jelly stock pot
1 large head of greens
½ tsp dried chilli flakes

2 x 50g portions dried rice noodles or
    2 x 150g sachets straight-to-wok
    wheat flour noodles
splash of soy sauce
splash of fish sauce
freshly ground black pepper, to taste

To serve
lime wedges
finely chopped spring onions
sriracha or other chilli sauce or DIY Garlic
    Chilli Oil (see page 61)

Finely chop the garlic and ginger. In a non-stick frying pan, fry the turkey mince in 1 teaspoon of the oil on a high heat, until it browns and starts to crisp.

In a separate large saucepan, heat the remaining oil and fry the garlic and ginger for a minute or so, until they just start to cook, then turn the heat off.

Put the kettle on to boil, and then make up 1 litre of stock using the stock cube or pot. Chop the greens into rough ribbons.

Drain any fat from the cooked turkey mince, then add the mince to the garlic and ginger pan, along with the chilli flakes and a good few twists of black pepper. Add the stock and turn the heat back on, bring to a simmer, then add the noodles, soy sauce and fish sauce. After a minute, add the greens. Cook until the noodles are done (around 5 minutes for dried noodles; 2–3 minutes for straight-to-wok noodles), and then ladle immediately into large bowls. Serve with lime wedges, spring onions and chilli sauce.

DIY Garlic Chilli Oil

You can buy a wide range of chilli oils in Asian supermarkets (with the exciting additions of things like fermented black beans or dried shrimps). But it's easy and relatively quick to make your own stuff and once you have, you'll probably find that your cupboard feels empty without it.

Drizzle it over a crispy, lacy-edged fried egg or into a simple soup for a spicy little kick – or put it to use in one of many of the recipes in this book.

This recipe makes enough to fill one of those small 100g jars that anchovies normally come in.

75ml vegetable oil

2 garlic cloves, sliced fairly thinly

1 tbsp dried chilli flakes

15 black peppercorns

Add the oil, garlic, chilli flakes and peppercorns to a small saucepan and cook on a medium heat for around 7 minutes. As the oil heats and reaches a simmer, the colour of the chilli will begin to infuse it – which is what you want.

Keep a very close eye on the pan to ensure nothing burns (the chilli will darken, but turn the heat down if it looks like it's approaching anything near a boil, and use your nose to detect the faintest whiff of burning too).

Remove from the heat the very second the garlic begins to colour to a golden brown. Don't just turn the heat off – move the pan to rest on a cool hob. When cool enough, decant into a clean, sterilised jar and seal. Store in the cupboard – it will keep for months.

Peanut Butter Noodles

It can be hard to look beyond the two classic, failsafe recipes for peanut butter. One: spread on hot toast. Two: use finger as utensil, and stick in jar. We've been trying to perfect a PB noodle combo for a while and have found that the spice and acidity of the chilli and lime are key in preventing everything from becoming too rich and claggy.

If you can't find limes (it happens, we know), use a tiny splash of vinegar (preferably rice or white wine vinegar) instead.

Serves 2

Preparation time: 5 minutes
Cooking time: 10–15 minutes

½ red onion
1 garlic clove
2 x 50g portions dried rice noodles or
    2 x 150g sachets straight-to-wok wheat
    flour noodles or 2 nests dried egg noodles
2 tbsp soy sauce

2 tbsp peanut butter (use crunchy or smooth
    according to taste or what's available)
2 tsp DIY Garlic Chilli Oil (see page 61),
    plus extra to serve
1½ tbsp groundnut oil or other neutral oil
juice of ½–1 lime
2 fried eggs, to serve (if hungry)
couple of lime wedges, to serve

Thinly slice the red onion, and finely chop the garlic.

If using dried noodles, put a pot of water on to boil. Cook the noodles according to the packet instructions. (If using straight-to-wok noodles, add them to the pan after you have cooked the onion and garlic.)

Combine the soy sauce, peanut butter, chilli oil and the juice of half a lime in a small bowl and mix together.

Put a frying pan on a high heat and add the groundnut oil. Add the onion and garlic and fry until golden and a bit crispy round the edges, but not burnt. Add the soy sauce mix to the pan and heat for 30 seconds.

Drain the cooked noodles, add to the pan and mix everything together (if the mix looks too dry, add a splash of water). Taste, and add the additional lime juice if you think it needs it. Serve, topping each portion with a fried egg, if you like. Serve with lime wedges and extra chilli oil.

Sesame Noodle Salad

Putting this together is probably quicker than ordering in, unless you live above a restaurant. Toast a big batch of sesame seeds and they'll keep in an airtight container for a couple of months. If you can get your hands on a rotisserie chicken or have some leftover from a roast then use that, otherwise any form of shop-bought cooked chicken from the chilled section will do nicely.

Serves 2

Preparation time: 10 minutes
Cooking time: 5 minutes (for noodles)

2 x 50g portions dried rice noodles or
  2 nests dried egg noodles
15cm piece of cucumber
4 spring onions
2 tbsp soy sauce
2 tbsp cider or white wine vinegar

2 tsp sesame oil
1 tsp toasted sesame seeds
1 tsp sugar
½ rotisserie chicken, cooled

To finish
handful of coriander, leaves picked
handful of mint, leaves picked
DIY Garlic Chilli Oil (see page 61)

Fill the kettle and put it on to boil. Add the dried rice noodles to a large heatproof bowl and pour over the boiling water. Cover with a tea towel to trap the steam, and leave for 5 minutes. (If using egg noodles, cook them according to the packet instructions.)

While you wait, thinly slice the cucumber and spring onions. Combine the soy sauce, vinegar, sesame oil, sesame seeds and sugar in a large bowl, mixing together well until the sugar dissolves.

Drain the noodles, shaking off as much excess water as possible (blot with kitchen towel, if necessary). Leave to cool – shred the chicken while you're waiting – then add the noodles, chicken, cucumber and spring onions to the bowl with the dressing and mix together.

Finish with coriander, mint and chilli oil, and serve.

Kidney Bean Curry

For some reason, kidney beans seem doomed to be seen as something you bung in at the end when making a chilli con carne. This creamy Indian-inspired curry seeks to redress kidney bean discrimination, by making them the star of the show.

Dried and soaked beans have a wonderful texture but aren't practical for time-sensitive midweek dinners, so we use tinned beans here, which become incredibly tender in a very short space of time.

Serves 4

Preparation time: 25 minutes
Cooking time: 40 minutes

For the kidney bean curry
½ green chilli
5cm piece of ginger
3 garlic cloves
1 onion
25g butter
1½ tbsp neutral oil, such as groundnut oil
½ tsp cumin seeds
1 tsp chilli powder
½ tsp ground cumin
½ tsp ground cinnamon
1 x 400g tin plum tomatoes or
    1 x 400g carton passata

2 x 400g tins red kidney beans
1 tsp salt
100ml semi-skimmed milk (or whatever milk
    you have in the fridge)

For the mint, cucumber and red onion raita
¼ cucumber
handful of mint leaves
¼ small red onion
1 x 170g pot natural Greek-style yoghurt
    (like Total)
good squeeze of lime juice
salt, to taste

To serve
300g busmati rice

First make your curry. Seed and chop the green chilli, peel the ginger and garlic and chop the onion into quarters. Add the ginger, garlic and onion to a small hand-held blender and whizz for a minute or so, or until everything is finely chopped. If you don't have a blender, use a pestle and mortar to make a ginger-garlic-onion paste with a bit of salt (this would be more traditional but also more arm-ache inducing), or just finely chop everything.

Add 10g of the butter and the oil to a cast-iron pot and put on a medium heat until the butter melts. Add the cumin seeds and cook for a minute or two, until they start to infuse and turn toasty. Next add the onion mix, cook for a couple of minutes, then add the ground spices and >

half of the green chilli. Cook for another 4 minutes. Add the tomatoes, crushing them with your hand as your pour them into the pan. Use up any juice left in the tin by adding a splash of water, giving it a swirl, and pouring in. Drain and rinse the kidney beans and add these too. Give everything a mix and taste. If it's spicy enough, don't add the rest of the green chilli. If it needs more kick, do. Also add the salt at this point. Cook, uncovered, on a low to medium heat for around 20 minutes.

While the curry cooks, put the rice on: rinse it, then add to a pan with double the amount of water to rice. Bring to the boil, then add a lid, turn down the heat and cook until all the water has been absorbed (around 20–25 minutes). Leave to stand with the lid still on for about 5 minutes, before serving.

While the rice is cooking, make the raita. Chop the cucumber in half lengthways, then into quarters, and cut out the seedy section from each strip. Cut the 4 strips into small, thin slices. Fincly chop the mint leaves and chop the red onion into small dice. Add everything to a bowl, along with the yoghurt. Give everything a good mix and add the lime juice and salt to taste.

Back to the curry: stir in the milk and the remaining butter and cook for a final 10 minutes. Serve with the cooked rice and the raita.

Twice-Cooked Aubergine, Two Ways

Nothing is more disappointing than a tough, chewy bit of aubergine — because nothing is more addictively delicious than aubergine that dissolves in your mouth. The double-pronged cooking method below is the fastest way we've found to get there. It's our experience that aubergines take as much oil as you throw at them — they're like that person at the end of a party, downing all the half empty glasses (sort of). We've tried to minimise the oiliness here, as there is something pleasingly abstemious(ish) about eating one vegetable with a simple sauce, and some plain rice or noodles.

Serves 2 (for a light dinner)

Preparation time: 10 minutes
Cooking time: 18 minutes

2 aubergines
4 tbsp olive oil

To serve (optional)
140g basmati rice, cooked, or 2 x 50g portions dried rice noodles, cooked

---

Preheat the oven to 200°C/gas 6.

Cut your aubergines in half lengthways, from stalk to bottom. Slice a deep crisscross pattern into the flesh of each half – don't cut all the way through to the skin, but go as close as you can. This will help them to cook more quickly.

Heat the oil in a frying pan on a medium to high heat. When hot, place the aubergine halves, cut sides down, in the pan and cook for around 6–8 minutes. If they are blackening too quickly, turn the heat down a bit. Flip over (tongs are useful here) and cook for a couple of minutes on the skin-side.

Remove from the pan to a baking tray. If you're making the Peanut Sesame Sauce (see overleaf), spread it over the aubergines now. If you're making the Spicy Vietnamese Sauce (see overleaf), leave them as is.

Bake for 10 minutes or until cooked – ovens and aubergines do vary, so give the flesh a poke to make sure they are cooked to melt-in-the-mouth perfection.

Spicy Vietnamese Sauce

*This packs a punch. Grated veg like carrot or cabbage can also be added
to bulk things up and add contrasting crunch.*

1 large garlic clove
1–1½ long red chillies (depending on
   hotness)
4 spring onions
juice of 2 limes
4 tsp fish sauce

1 tsp granulated sugar
3 tbsp water

To finish
large handful of coriander, leaves picked
large handful of mint, leaves picked

While the aubergines finish cooking in the oven, finely dice or crush the garlic, seed and finely
chop the chillies and thinly slice the spring onions, then mix in a bowl with the lime juice, fish
sauce, sugar and water.

If you're having cooked rice or noodles, make a little bed of these under the aubergines, then the
sauce can trickle down. Pour the sauce over the warm aubergine halves and finish with the herbs.

Peanut Sesame Sauce

This isn't going to win any beauty contests, but it does taste good.

1 garlic clove
6cm piece of ginger, peeled
2 tbsp smooth peanut butter
2 tsp sriracha chilli sauce
1 tbsp sesame oil
splash of soy sauce

3 tbsp water

To finish
large handful of toasted sesame seeds
finely chopped spring onions

Finely dice or crush the garlic and grate the ginger, then mix with all the other ingredients in a bowl. Spread the mixture (a pastry brush comes in handy here) over the cut sides of the aubergine halves, before putting them in the oven for their final 10 minutes of cooking.

If you're having cooked rice or noodles, add these to your plates first, then top with the aubergine halves, and finish with sesame seeds and spring onions.

THE ALTERNATIVE TAKEAWAY

Sardine Banh Mi

In Vietnam, we've heard that these are made using sardines packed in a special spicy tomato sauce, but John West's finest works just fine. If you want to up the heat, add a bit more chilli sauce, or even a sprinkling of dried chilli flakes. Beetroot is unorthodox, but acts as a ready-made pickle, cutting through the fish. The perfect quick dinner for one for a night in on the sofa.

Serves 1

Preparation time: 10 minutes
Cooking time: 12 minutes

1 small carrot, julienned or grated (see method below)
5 slices of pickled beetroot, cut into thin matchsticks
1 spring onion, cut into thirds widthways, then sliced into thin sticks lengthways

pinch of salt
1 tsp rice or cider vinegar
1 ready-to-bake baguette or small fresh baguette
1 x 120g tin sardines in tomato sauce
good squirt of mayonnaise
good squirt of chilli sauce (sriracha is our favourite, but use whatever type you like)
handful of coriander, leaves picked

Preheat the oven to 220°C/gas 7.

While the oven is heating, make your pickled salad. For the carrot, use a serrated julienne peeler if you have one, or a box grater on the rough/thickest side if you don't. Combine the carrot with the beetroot and spring onion sticks in a bowl, then add a pinch of salt and the vinegar and give everything a good mix together. Leave to the side.

If using a ready-to-bake baguette, bake it for 12 minutes or until golden and crisp. Remove and leave to cool before slicing the baguette in half lengthways.

Add the tomatoey sardines to the bottom of the baguette, removing the spines and any large bones and breaking the fish into large pieces using a fork. Spread the top of the baguette with the mayonnaise, then add some chilli sauce to the sardines, before topping with the pickled salad and the coriander. Sandwich together and enjoy.

Spiced Lamb Breads

Quick to make, these lamb breads can be enjoyed as luxury wraps, or baked, then sliced and shared. You will have to adapt the method according to how lean your lamb is. Whilst you are unlikely to find whole pomegranates in your local mini supermarket, they are now widely sold seeded in convenient little packets in the 'meal deal' section somewhere between the sliced pineapple and Dairylea Dunkers. Otherwise, we have noticed Turkish and Italian-owned smaller shops sometimes sell them.

Serves 2 as a light main course or 4 as a starter

Preparation time: 12 minutes
Cooking time: 15–18 minutes

1 tbsp olive oil, plus extra for drizzling
200g lamb mince
2 garlic cloves, crushed
1 tsp ground cumin
½ tsp ground allspice
½ tsp ground cinnamon
½ tsp ground coriander
1 star anise

2 large flour tortillas
handful of baby spinach leaves, rinsed
1 tbsp pine nuts
1 tsp flaked almonds
pinch of sumac (optional)
salt and freshly ground black pepper

To finish
2 tsp pomegranate seeds
natural or Greek-style natural yoghurt

Preheat the oven to 150°C/gas 2.

Place the oil in a non-stick frying pan on a medium to high heat, and after a minute, add the lamb mince. Cook until the meat begins to brown and 'pop' in parts. Add the garlic and sprinkle over some pepper. If the pan appears too dry, add some more oil, or conversely, remove the excess oil if your lamb is very fatty. Follow with the spices and continue to cook for a few more minutes.

Lay the tortillas on a baking tray. Divide the lamb mix between the two, removing the star anise. Sprinkle over some salt and top with the spinach leaves, pine nuts and flaked almonds. Finish with a drizzle of oil and a sprinkle of sumac, if using. Bake for 5 minutes.

Remove from the oven and top with pomegranate seeds and a smattering of natural yoghurt to finish. Serve immediately.

Yam Dumplings with Red Lentil Curry

Thanks to the wonderfully diverse cultures which make up the UK, many metropolitan cornershops sell an assortment of beautiful yet unfamiliar fruit and veg: whether cassava, durian or Japanese turnip, we should make more use of these ingredients; scary-looking though some might be, we are incredibly fortunate to have such food from around the world on our doorsteps.

This recipe attempts to de-mystify yams: those strange, enormous, intimidating black vegetables. Granted, they are loved by millions of people around the globe and sustain many peoples with calories and comfort, but for some British palates, their starchy texture can be a challenge.

Fufu is a popular way of serving yam. The method is pretty well identical to making mashed potato; the yam is then traditionally shaped into balls and used to scoop up stew and curry to be eaten with fingers. In this recipe, the yam balls are fried to add colour and served as 'dumplings' on rice, with the curry sauce spooned on top.

Serves 6 — 8

Preparation time: 30 minutes
Cooking time: 30 minutes

For the dumplings
350g yam
1 x 400g tin chickpeas, drained and rinsed
1 egg, beaten
1 tsp dried chilli flakes
1 spring onion, thinly sliced
sunflower oil, for frying

For the red lentil curry
3 tbsp olive oil
seeds of 4 green cardamom pods
2 onions
2 tsp ground cumin

1 tsp ground coriander
1 tsp ground turmeric
1 tsp cayenne pepper
thumb-sized piece of ginger, peeled and
    minced or finely chopped
2–3 garlic cloves, crushed
2 x 400g tins chopped tomatoes
250g red lentils, rinsed
stalks from 20g coriander, finely chopped
juice of 1 lemon
salt and freshly ground black pepper

To serve
300g basmati rice
handful of coriander leaves, chopped
natural yoghurt

To make the dumplings, peel the yam using a sharp knife (we found an ordinary peeler to be ineffective on the tough brown skin) and chop into 2.5cm chunks. Place in a colander and rinse under a cold tap for a minute. Add to a large saucepan and cover with water. Bring to the boil and leave to simmer until tender, usually about 15 minutes, then drain.

Meanwhile, make your red lentil curry. Heat the olive oil in a large pan and add the cardamom seeds. Chop the onions and add to the pan. Soften slowly, putting the lid on from time to time, then add the ground spices, ginger and garlic. After a minute, add the tomatoes and 1 ½ cans of water, followed by the lentils and chopped coriander stalks. Season with salt and pepper, and leave to simmer, partially covered, for 20 minutes, or until the lentils are cooked. Keep warm.

Now continue making your dumplings. Place the cooked, drained yam in a large mortar (or pound-proof bowl) and pound using a pestle, wooden spoon or potato masher until you have something that resembles mashed potato. Alternatively, you could blitz the lot in a food processor (if you own one).

In a separate bowl, purée the chickpeas to a smooth-ish paste with the egg, using a hand-held blender or otherwise. Combine with the mashed yam, along with the chilli flakes, spring onion and salt and pepper. Form the mix into golf ball-sized balls, and then fry in batches in sunflower oil (squashing them with a spatula in the pan to ensure they cook through), turning once, until golden. Each batch usually takes 3 4 minutes.

About 30 minutes before you are ready to serve, place a pan of salted water on to boil, and cook your rice according to the packet instructions, then drain (if necessary). Finish the lentil curry by adding the lemon juice and giving it a final blast to heat through.

Serve the dumplings on the cooked rice, with the lentil curry spooned over. Finish with a smattering of chopped coriander leaves and natural yoghurt.

Virtuous Vegetable Rice Bowl

This colourful, cheering dinner leaves you satisfied without feeling like you're going to immediately pass out on the sofa (unlike, say, a Pepperoni Passion with extra garlic dip…).

Inspired by the Korean staple, bibimbap, the dressing (an homage to the traditional fermented chilli paste, gochujang) is key, but otherwise tailor the recipe to what you like or can find. Leeks, broccoli, courgettes, kale (steamed), mushrooms and red cabbage (raw) would all work well in place of some or all of the veg listed below.

You can of course use white rice or add protein in the form of diced tofu, cooked prawns or shredded meat. The egg can be soft or hard-boiled, even poached; though the crunchy edges of the olive oil fried egg provide an enjoyable textural contrast to the other ingredients, if you're into that kind of thing.

Though it looks long, this recipe is not very labour intensive. You will need to use a small saucepan and a frying pan, but we've suggested reusing these to save on washing up.

Serves 2

Preparation time: 15 minutes
Cooking time: 30 minutes

For the rice bowl
150g brown rice
300ml water

For the dressing
4cm piece of ginger, peeled
1 large garlic clove, peeled
2cm piece of red chilli, seeded
2 tbsp soy sauce
3 tbsp thick chilli sauce like sriracha
1 tsp sesame oil
juice of 1 lime

For the veg
1 carrot
10cm piece of cucumber
2 ready-cooked beetroot
1 avocado
200g spinach, rinsed

To finish
1½ tbsp olive oil
2 eggs
salt, to taste
dried chilli flakes, to taste
1 tsp toasted sesame seeds (see overleaf)
2 spring onions, finely chopped

Rinse the rice, put it in a pan (for which you have a lid) with the water and bring to the boil, then put the lid on and turn the heat down. Cook until the water has been fully absorbed (a glass lid comes in handy here) – it should take around 20–25 minutes), then turn the heat off and leave to stand for 5 minutes.

While the rice is cooking, do your prep work. Add all the dressing ingredients to a hand-held blender and whizz until the ginger, garlic and chilli are fully broken down. Set aside.

For the veg, use a julienne peeler (or you could use a coarse grater) to cut the carrot into thin little matchsticks. Cut the cucumber into 4 pieces lengthways, remove the seeded middles, then cut into small chunks. Cut the beets into slightly chunkier matchsticks. Halve, stone and slice the avocado (while in its skin) into thin segments, then push or scoop out the segments.

By this point the rice should be done. Add the rice to the bowls you're going to serve in. Wilt down the spinach in the pan you used for the rice (give it a quick wipe if you want) – the water from rinsing it will steam it – then squeeze out any excess water.

Top the rice with the steamed spinach, the carrot, cucumber, beetroot and avocado, arranging each type of veg around the bowls in separate sections, like a pie chart.

For the pièce de resistance (i.e. the eggs), get a frying pan (the one you used to toast the sesame seeds – see below) nice and hot. Add the olive oil and once hot, crack in the eggs, spacing them so they don't merge. Immediately season with salt and chilli flakes. Cook to your personal taste – we like the edges to get brown and crispy, while the yolk remains runny (this happens pretty quickly).

Crown the rice and veg bowls with the eggs, scatter over the toasted sesame seeds and spring onions, and serve the dressing on the side to add as you like.

TOASTING SESAME SEEDS

Dry toast the sesame seeds in a frying pan on a low heat, keeping an eagle eye on them to ensure that they don't burn (this sounds obvious, but if you are anything like us, you will put them on, start doing something else, and immediately forget about them, until you smell burning). Decant into a small bowl, until needed.

Papaya Salad

We don't always want meat on a weeknight, but more often than not we do want something packed with flavour and goodness. This papaya salad is a delicious way of getting that aromatic healthy fix without the deep-fried rolls you'd inevitably be ordering alongside it if you were in a Vietnamese restaurant.

Make this whenever you see papaya in your local cornershop or mini supermarket as it's an exotic treat and you only need a couple. Asian supermarkets usually sell green (unripe) papaya, which also works here – just prepare differently as directed. If you feel you need something slightly more substantial, you can stuff the salad into a toasted pitta with some mayonnaise if no one is watching.

Serves 2

Preparation time: 10 minutes
Cooking time: 5 minutes

For the salad
250g green beans
500g papayas (2 smallish ones)
25g fresh mint
25g fresh basil
150g cherry tomatoes
20g salted peanuts

For the dressing
2 tbsp olive oil or sesame oil
juice of ½ lime
splash of fish sauce
splash of rice wine vinegar
1 garlic clove, crushed
salt and freshly ground black pepper

For the salad, place a small saucepan filled with salted water on a medium to high heat, and top and tail the green beans.

Peel the papayas, then chop in half and scoop out the seeds. If they are ripe and orange, scoop out the flesh using a spoon, otherwise (if green) grate into strips using a cheese grater or julienning tool (available from many Chinese supermarkets for a few quid).

Add the green beans to the hopefully by now boiling water and blanch for 3–4 minutes. When the time is up, drain in a colander and run under the cold tap.

Pick the mint and basil leaves off the stalks and roughly chop. Slice the cherry tomatoes in half, and chop up the peanuts. Once the green beans are cool, drain and then pat them dry on a clean tea towel.

Take a salad bowl, add all of the dressing ingredients and whisk together with a fork. Taste to check the seasoning and adjust with more lime juice and/or pepper. Be sparing with extra salt as your peanuts are salted.

Add the papaya, green beans, cherry tomatoes and herbs to the bowl and toss in the dressing. Dish out on to plates and finish with a sprinkling of chopped peanuts.

THE CATCH-UP DINNER

Weekends are few and far between, and unless you're pretty organised, you can easily find yourself going for weeks, then months, without seeing the dear friends that revitalise, inspire and calm you. This is where the mid-week catch-up dinner comes in: meals cooked for one or two friends, often spontaneously organised. You want to make the effort to deviate from your normal comfortable rota of pesto pasta, chilli con carne, cheese on toast (and repeat), but in a way, the food is almost incidental.

What follows in this chapter is a series of easily put together dishes that everyone will enjoy. Unlike most of the recipes in 'The Unplanned Dinner Party', they are the kind of things you might cook for the people you really don't mind delegating the odd job to: chopping or grating, laying the table, organising your recycling (just joking about the last one: Caroline was once tasked with taking out the rubbish by Sophie's husband – a delegation we don't suggest you extend to your dinner companions).

The point is that your guest(s) haven't come to be impressed, or to sample the latest twenty-nine ingredient recipe from the Sunday supplements: they're just happy to see you and to be eating some nice grub they haven't had to shop for and make themselves. So don't worry too much, and allow them to get stuck in (helping you), before they tuck in.

Aubergine Lahmacun

Lahmacun is a Turkish flatbread, similar to a pizza, usually made with minced lamb. This (loose) veggie interpretation uses smoky aubergine instead. We normally grill the aubergines and peppers directly over the hob – if you don't have a gas hob, use the grill function in your oven instead.

Note that this is a knife and fork job: a tortilla base is structurally unsound and will undoubtedly collapse if you attempt to slice and eat with your hands. This is a light dinner, so if you wanted to add an egg – boiled, poached or fried – to each pizza, then we wouldn't stop you.

Makes 2

Preparation time: around 15 minutes
Cooking time: 20 minutes

2 medium aubergines or 1 large aubergine
2 red peppers
¼ small red cabbage
½ red onion
2 tbsp red wine vinegar
pinch of salt, plus extra to taste

couple of handfuls of parsley
2 tbsp pine nuts or walnuts
1 large garlic clove, crushed
2 tbsp olive oil
2 tortilla wraps
½ x 170g pot natural Greek-style
   yoghurt (like Total)
sprinkling of dried chilli flakes
2 lemon quarters

Preheat the oven to 150°C/gas 2.

You may want to line the base of your hob with foil to save on cleaning later. Fire up all four gas rings and place an aubergine and red pepper on each (or use a preheated hot grill to do this bit, if you don't have a gas hob). Have metal tongs at the ready to turn them every so often – you want to cook them until they are charred on the outside but meltably juicy within (give them a prod with the tongs to gauge this). This will take around 15 minutes. Thank you Yotam Ottolenghi for bringing this method into the authors' kitchens, forever ensuring our aubergine flesh is imbibed with a delicious smoky flavour...

While you're waiting (and making sure that nothing is catching on fire), use a mandoline or sharp knife to finely shred the cabbage and slice the onion, then place in a bowl with the red wine vinegar and a pinch of salt. Set aside.

When the aubergines and peppers are done, move them to a baking tray and leave to cool. While you're waiting, chop the parsley, and toast the pine nuts in a small pan on a low heat for a few minutes until lightly browned all over. Remove and cool.

When the veg are cool, peel off the charred skin and remove any seeds and stalks. Rip or slice the peppers into long shreds and put in a bowl. Add the ripped aubergine flesh to another bowl and mix in the garlic and oil, plus salt to taste, giving everything a good mash.

Wrap the tortillas in foil and heat in the oven for a minute or two – so they warm up but not so that they go really crisp. Take out and pop on two plates.

Create your lahmacun by smoothing the aubergine mix over the wraps as you would tomato sauce, then topping with pieces of red pepper, blobs of yoghurt, the pickled cabbage and onion and a sprinkling of pine nuts, parsley and chilli flakes. Finish by squeezing over the lemon quarters.

Smoked Salmon Baked Eggs

This much-adored meal has been upgraded from brunch status in our households. It takes no time at all to prepare and manages to exude both comfort and class, like a shiny brogue.

You will need to crack out the ovenproof ramekins for this and serve with plenty of buttered toast.

Makes 6 pots

Preparation time: 8 minutes
Cooking time: 12 minutes

For the baked eggs
knob of butter, for greasing
6 eggs
6 tbsp crème fraîche
120g smoked salmon slices, chopped
6 sprigs of dill or a few snipped chives
salt and freshly ground black pepper

For the salad
250g ready-cooked beetroot
1 x 60g bag rocket or spinach leaves
2 tbsp olive oil
1 tsp red wine vinegar
2 tsp lemon juice

buttered toast (lots), to serve

Preheat the oven to 180°C/gas 4.

For the baked eggs, grease the inside of 6 ovenproof ramekins with the butter, then crack an egg into each. Add a tablespoon of crème fraîche to each, along with the smoked salmon, shared between the 6 ramekins. Top each with a little sprig of dill (or a sprinkle of chives) and a grind of black pepper. Bake for 10-12 minutes until the egg whites have set but the yolks are still wobbly.

Meanwhile, for the salad, cut each beet into 8 wedges and place in a bowl with the rocket leaves, oil, red wine vinegar and lemon juice. Mix well, then add seasoning to taste.

Serve the egg ramekins on plates as they will be very hot, with the salad on the side, and plenty of buttered toast for dunking into the oozy goodness.

Fried Eggs with Cured Ham and Paprika-Spiced Potatoes

Enhanced ham, egg and chips. The trick here is not to scrimp on the charcuterie. Most mini supermarkets stock Parma ham. Get a standard 70g packet per person.

Serves 4

Preparation time: 10 minutes
Cooking time: 20 minutes

For the tomato salsa
4 ripe tomatoes
olive oil, for drizzling
lime juice or red wine vinegar, for drizzling
½ small red onion
½ garlic clove, finely chopped
pinch of dried chilli flakes

For the paprika-spiced potatoes
500g potatoes
1 tbsp olive oil, plus extra for frying
sprinkling of smoked paprika
salt and freshly ground black pepper

280g parma ham
knobs of butter, for frying
8 eggs
buttered toast and chilli sauce, to serve

Preheat the oven 220°C/gas 7. For the paprika-spiced potatoes, chop the potatoes into 1cm dice, then place in a roasting tin, drizzle over the oil, sprinkle over the smoked paprika and salt and pepper, and mix to coat evenly. Roast for 10–15 minutes, scraping the potatoes off the bottom of the tin with a metal spatula every so often, until they are golden and crispy in bits.

Meanwhile, make your salsa. Roughly chop the tomatoes and place in a bowl. Drizzle with some oil and lime juice (or red wine vinegar), and season with plenty of salt and some pepper. Finely chop the onion and add to the salsa, along with the garlic and chilli flakes, mixing well.

When your potatoes are nearing a state of readiness, prepare the plates, spooning tomato salsa and some ham on to each. Finally, attend to your eggs: place 2 large frying pans on a medium heat and add a knob of butter and a drizzle of oil to each one. When the butter and oil are bubbling, fry the eggs until cooked to your liking. If you only have one frying pan, do the eggs in two batches.

Immediately transfer the fried eggs to the prepared plates, spooning the roast spiced potatoes alongside, and serve with buttered toast and chilli sauce.

Artichoke Linguine

Simple, speedy and sophisticated. Enjoy with a lovely glass of Sauvignon Blanc. Simply double or triple the ingredients if you wish to cook this for more people.

Serves 2

Preparation time: 5 minutes
Cooking time: 12 minutes

200g linguine
2 tbsp olive oil
1 garlic clove

1 x 400g tin or jar artichoke hearts, drained
    and finely chopped
1 egg, at room temperature
4 tbsp grated Parmesan
snipped chives, to taste
salt and freshly ground black pepper

Put a pan of salted water on to boil. Add the pasta once the water is bubbling and cook according to the packet instructions.

Meanwhile in a separate, extra-large pan, heat the oil. Finely chop the garlic and add to the pan, then follow with the artichokes. Leave to cook through on a medium to low heat for 3–4 minutes.

Crack the egg into a little bowl and whisk lightly. When your pasta is al dente, drain and add to the pan of artichokes, along with a splash of the cooking water. Turn the heat off and stir in the Parmesan, along with the beaten egg. Combine quickly for a minute, before seasoning with salt and pepper, along with a snip or two of chives. Enjoy.

Mushroom Ragu

Traditional meat ragus take hours of slow, patient simmering – perfect for a lazy weekend pootling around the house doing chores, but less so during the week when you need a speedier supper. This mushroom version is lighter but still comforting – especially when paired with creamy mash (which also serves to thicken up the sauce when on the plate).

If you really fancy a bit of meat, add some lardons, or small pieces of bacon, to the pan and cook for 5 minutes before adding the mushrooms.

Serves 2 generously

Preparation time: 20 minutes
Cooking time: 40 minutes

For the mushroom ragu
1 onion
3 garlic cloves
1 carrot
1 stick celery
1 tbsp olive oil
20g butter
400g button mushrooms
2 sprigs of thyme
2 sprigs of rosemary

1 tsp tomato purée
75ml red wine (do what you will with the rest of the bottle)
120ml hot vegetable stock (like bouillon) – add more water, if needed
salt and freshly ground black pepper

For the creamy mash
1 large or 2 medium potatoes
15g butter
splash of milk
1 tbsp crème fraîche or natural yoghurt

Finely chop the onion and garlic. Dice the carrot and celery into similar-sized pieces. Heat the oil and butter in a casserole pot and add the onion, garlic, carrot and celery, along with a pinch of salt, sautéing for around 15 minutes, until softened and starting to turn a bit golden.

Chop the mushrooms into quarters (or halves if they are especially small). Add to the pan, along with the herb sprigs, and cook until the mushrooms start to soften. Season with pepper, then add the tomato purée, stir and fry off for 3 minutes. Add the wine and cook on a high heat until it reduces down – for around 10 minutes. Add the hot stock and, lowering the heat slightly, cook, uncovered, for another 10–15 minutes, until the broth is fragrant and slightly reduced, and the mushrooms are tender.

While your ragu is bubbling away, make the creamy mash. Peel the potato(es) and chop into evenly-sized, small-ish chunks. Cover with water in a saucepan, and bring to the boil. Cook until tender, or easily pierced with a knife. Drain, then add the butter, milk and crème fraîche and mash together until smooth. Add salt to taste.

Check the ragu for seasoning and adjust to taste, then serve with a pile of the creamy mash.

Veggie Mezze Menu of Joy

Who doesn't love a composite meal where the foundations are copious amounts of bread, dips and tasty sides? Here, we've suggested a spread including a fair few of our favourite dishes to create our own Mezze Platter, however, you by no means need to make all of them. If you're up to the challenge, you could make all of the dishes in advance barring the Spiced Creamed Spinach and the Courgette and Halloumi Rolls.

The pièce de resistance is the Kashke Bademyam, a delicious Persian aubergine dish, so do prioritise that if you can, and mix and match with whatever else you have strength for. Aim for at least four dishes, alongside the usual offerings of olives, fruit and nuts.

Many of the elements should of course be bought ready-made, moreover don't hesitate to delegate grating and chopping tasks to your fellow diners: par for the course if one is being cooked for on a 'school' night. Jazz up shop-bought houmous with extra-virgin olive oil, lemon juice and a sprinkling of smoked paprika. And ask whoever lives closest to the nicest bakery to bring along some lovely bread, Turkish if you can get it, otherwise bake-at-home ciabatta does the trick nicely.

Menu serves 4 — 6

Kashke Bademyam

Preparation time: 10 minutes
Cooking time: 30 minutes, plus resting

20g butter
1 onion
1 cinnamon stick
3 aubergines
extra-virgin olive oil, for drizzling

juice of 1 lemon
3 tbsp natural yoghurt
1 garlic clove
20g walnuts
20g pine nuts
handful of mint
handful of parsley
salt and freshly ground black pepper

Melt the butter in a frying pan. Thinly slice the onion and add to the pan, along with the cinnamon stick, then slowly fry until the onion is thin, sweet and a little crispy. Leave to cook gently while you attend to the aubergines.

If you have a gas hob, turn three burners on to a medium heat, then place each aubergine directly on the flames (you may want to line the base of the hob with foil to save on cleaning later). If you don't have a gas hob, pierce the skin of the aubergines 4 or 5 times with a fork or knife and either bake in a preheated oven at 180°C/gas 4 for 45 minutes, or in a microwave on full power for 10–20 minutes depending on the aubergine size. You won't get that chargrilled taste but you will have much less cleaning to do afterwards.

Turn the aubergines round occasionally and cook until they are floppy and cooked through (usually about 15 minutes on the hob). Place in a colander and leave until cool enough to handle. Either peel off the skin or, using a knife or spoon, scrape away the flesh and return to the colander, giving it a squeeze before leaving to drain for 10 minutes.

Chop the drained aubergine flesh before placing in a bowl, then drizzle over some lovely oil. Add half of the lemon juice, a tablespoon of the yoghurt and season with salt and pepper. Crush or finely grate in the garlic. Taste and adjust with more oil, salt or lemon juice if needs be.

Roughly chop the walnuts. Add about a third of the walnuts to the aubergine mix, together with about a third of the pine nuts, mixing well. Discard the stalks from the mint and parsley and roughly chop the leaves, then add about a third of each to the aubergine mix, holding the rest back for the topping.

Finally and separately, mix together the remaining lemon juice and yoghurt in a small bowl, and add a little salt, then drizzle over the aubergine mix. Sprinkle over the remaining nuts and herbs, followed by the buttery crispy onions (discard the cinnamon stick). Finish with a final drizzle of oil, and serve with plenty of bread and crudités for dipping or spreading.

Carrot Salad

Preparation time: 5 minutes

3 carrots
squeeze or two of lemon juice

1 tbsp olive oil
1 tbsp chopped fresh parsley
1 tsp poppy seeds (optional)

Simply peel then grate the carrots, place in a bowl and drizzle over the lemon juice and oil. Finish with a few snips of parsley and some poppy seeds, if using. ›

Tomato Salad

Preparation time: 5 minutes

250g ripe tomatoes or cherry tomatoes
½ red onion
olive oil, for drizzling

sumac or dried chilli flakes, to taste
squeeze of lemon juice
salt and freshly ground black pepper
few basil leaves, to finish

Finely chop the tomatoes and onion (simply quarter the cherry tomatoes, if using). Place in a bowl and sprinkle over some salt and pepper, oil, sumac or chilli flakes and a squeeze of lemon juice. Finish with a few basil leaves.

Courgette and Halloumi Rolls

Preparation time: 5 minutes
Cooking time: 10 minutes

3 courgettes
10g butter

1 x 225g packet halloumi, cut into
   bite-sized pieces
salt and freshly ground black pepper

Using a peeler or sharp knife, slice the courgettes lenghtways from the top to the bottom in long, thin strips as wide as possible.

Then, place a frying pan on a medium heat and melt the butter. Add the halloumi pieces in batches and fry until golden brown all over.

To serve take a courgette strip, roll it up around a piece of cooked halloumi and secure with a cocktail stick. Continue until you have used up all the halloumi. (Any leftover courgette will be lovely in a salad.) Serve immediately.

Spiced Creamed Spinach

Preparation time: 5 minutes
Cooking time: 25 minutes

15g butter
1 onion
15g plain flour
250ml milk

400g spinach leaves, rinsed
20g pine nuts
generous grating of nutmeg
pinch of ground allspice
¼ tsp finely grated lemon zest
salt and finely ground black pepper

Melt the butter in a large saucepan on a medium to low heat. Finely chop the onion and add to the pan. Cook, while stirring from time to time, for about 7 minutes, until the onion is soft and translucent and has acquired a sweet taste.

Sprinkle the flour over the cooked onion and stir continuously with a wooden spoon or spatula for 1-2 minutes on a medium heat. Still stirring, trickle in the milk in a continuous flow and gradually bring to the boil. Turn down the heat, season with salt and pepper, then incorporate the spinach leaves and mix as best as you can to coat them in your sauce.

Put the lid on and turn the heat down to low. Cook for about 10 minutes until the leaves have wilted, stirring regularly to coat them in sauce (the heat should be low enough to prevent any catching). If you feel the sauce is too runny, remove the lid, turn up the heat a little to evaporate some excess liquid, before mixing in the pine nuts, nutmeg, allspice and lemon zest. Serve immediately. >

Garlicky Raita

Preparation time: 5 minutes

10cm piece of cucumber
300ml natural yoghurt
handful of mint leaves, chopped

squeeze of lemon juice
¼ garlic clove, crushed
olive oil, for drizzling
pinch of smoked paprika
salt and freshly ground black pepper

Finely chop the cucumber, discarding any large seeds and juice, and place in a serving bowl with the yoghurt and almost all the mint. Mix in a squeeze of lemon juice, the garlic and some salt and pepper. Finish with a drizzle of oil, the smoked paprika, and the remaining chopped mint.

Beetroot and Feta Dip

Preparation time: 7 minutes

250g ready-cooked beetroot
1 x 400g tin butter beans, drained and rinsed
3 tbsp sour cream
juice of ½ lemon

dash of extra-virgin olive oil
salt and freshly ground black pepper

To finish
2 tbsp crumbled feta cheese
chopped fresh parsley

Place the beets, beans, sour cream, lemon juice and oil in a bowl and blend together using a hand-held stick blender until you have a lovely-looking smooth-ish pink dip. Taste to check the seasoning and make any necessary adjustments. Finish with crumbled feta and choppped parsley.

Orange Dessert

Preparation time: 7 minutes

Give an orange fruit salad (peel, de-pith and thinly slice 3 large oranges) a simple Persian twist by sprinkling over some ground cardamom (remove the seeds from a green pod, and crush using a pestle and mortar) and orange blossom water or rosewater. Chopped mint leaves would also add aromatic value.

Kedgeree

Kedgeree is traditionally made using smoked haddock, however, unless you're lucky, this is pretty tricky to source locally. This hasn't put us off from crafting our own version of this lovely buttery, spiced rice dish though, as un-smoked white fish such as cod or pollock isn't a problem to find in mini supermarkets and it all tastes rather lovely. The key is juggling the different cooking times.

If you really miss that characteristic smoky flavour, you could use smoked salmon or mackerel in this dish: omit the poaching at the beginning and use fish stock to cook the rice instead. Flake in the fish about 5 minutes towards the end of the rice cooking time to heat through.

For a truly cornershop version, omit the fish and just use extra eggs, as the spiced rice really holds its own in this dish. You'll probably have to call it Eggeree though…

Serves 4

Preparation time: 30 minutes
Cooking time: 30 minutes

300g basmati rice
2 fish stock cubes
300g white fish fillets
6 eggs
75g butter
1 onion
1 cinnamon stick

½ tsp ground turmeric
1½ tsp curry powder
seeds from 2 green cardamom pods, crushed
freshly ground black pepper, to taste

To finish and serve
handful of parsley leaves, chopped
handful of coriander leaves, chopped
lemon wedges

Rinse the rice in plenty of cold water, then leave to soak in a bowl filled with warm water for about 30 minutes. Begin the stages below after 10–15 minutes have elapsed.

Bring 2 pans of water to the boil: one big one with 1 litre of fish stock (made using the stock cubes) and one smaller one filled with plain water. Add the white fish to the stock, reducing the heat to a simmer, and poach for about 5–6 minutes. Add the eggs to the boiling water and cook for 6 minutes. When the fish flesh is flaky and opaque, remove from the pan using a spatula, discard the skin and set the flesh aside, reserving the stock – you will use this liquid to cook the rice. Drain the boiled eggs and then set them aside.

While the fish is poaching and the eggs are boiling, melt the butter in a large, deep frying pan on a medium to low heat. Thinly slice the onion and add to the pan, along with the cinnamon stick. Cook gently for 15 minutes until the onion goes golden in bits, stirring occasionally, and then add the remaining spices.

Now, drain your rice and add to the onion mix, and with the heat turned up, stir continuously so the rice soaks up the buttery spicy goodness. Turn the heat back on under the fish stock and after a minute, ladle 450ml into the rice pan. Let the rice bubble for a minute or so, before turning the heat right down, covering with foil or a lid if the pan has one, and cooking for a further 7 minutes. Check the pan is not too dry after 5 minutes and add a little more fish stock if so. After the 7 minutes have elapsed, taste the rice to check it is cooked. When ready, remove the foil, flake in the cooked fish and stir for a minute to heat through, then turn the heat off.

Peel then quarter the eggs and pop on top of the rice dish. Sprinkle over some black pepper and finish with the parsley and coriander. Serve immediately with lemon wedges.

Frank's Tuna Melt

Sometimes nothing beats a sandwich for dinner. Our friend Frank and his pals used to make this tuna mix for staff lunches at the restaurant where they worked, buying all the ingredients from the cornershop down the road. The resulting big bowl of tuna is enough to feed a lunchtime restaurant crew, or some friends.

Makes 4 — 6

Preparation time: 10 minutes (including pickle making)
Cooking time: 5 minutes (for cheese melting and sandwich toasting)

For the Sichuan-style cucumber pickle
1 cucumber
1 tbsp table salt
1 garlic clove
1 tsp caster sugar
2 tbsp DIY Garlic Chilli Oil (see page 61)
1½ tbsp rice vinegar (or cider vinegar)
½ tsp sesame oil
splash of soy sauce

For the tuna
2 spring onions
1 long red chilli

4 x 120g tins tuna in brine
1 x 198g tin sweetcorn (get the salt-free type if you can)
1 heaped tbsp mayonnaise, plus extra for spreading
good glug of olive oil
juice of 1½ lemons
2 tbsp Thai sweet chilli sauce
bunch of coriander, leaves picked and finely shredded
pinch of salt
lots of freshly ground black pepper

For the melts
enough bread for however many sandwiches you're making (8–12 slices)
sliced or grated Emmenthal or another meltable cheese of your choosing

Preheat the oven to 180°C/gas 4. Line a baking tray with parchment paper.

For the pickle, cut the cucumber in half widthways, then cut each half into 4 pieces lengthways. Cut or scoop out the seedy middle and discard. Cut each quarter in half again, and then into small (about 3cm) chunks. Put the cucumber chunks into a colander, sprinkle with the table salt and leave for 15 minutes.

Meanwhile, for the pickle dressing, mince or crush the garlic, then combine with all the other ingredients in a medium-sized bowl (you'll use this for serving later). Set aside.

For the tuna, thinly slice the spring onions and seed and finely dice the chilli. Drain the tuna and sweetcorn and mix together in a bowl with the spring onions, chilli and all the 'wet' ingredients. Add the coriander last, then season with a pinch of salt and plenty of black pepper. Have a taste and add more of anything as you think necessary.

For the melts, put half of the bread slices on to the lined baking tray and spread each with a thin layer of mayo, then top evenly with the tuna mix, pushing it out until it reaches the crusts. Top with the cheese.

Bake in the oven until the cheese has melted, then top each with another slice of bread and bake for another couple of minutes so that each whole sandwich is warmed through.

Meanwhile, finish the pickle. Rinse the cucumber, then drain and pat dry. Add to the dressing, giving it all a good mix together. Let it stand for a couple of minutes, then mix again.

Serve the warm tuna melts with the pickle alongside. You won't have leftovers.

Anchovy, Onion and Potato Gratin

Our version of the Swedish Jansson's Temptation; just the ticket when the last of the leaves have fallen and there's a nip in the air. Cream, potatoes, onion, anchovy (in pretty much that order): what's not to like? Unsurprisingly, given its largely yellow or white ingredients, this is very rich, so a green salad is a good accompaniment and the tiniest of nods (more of a sort of twitch) to health.

Serves 4 — 6

Preparation time: 15 minutes
Cooking time: 1 hour 5 minutes
   (45 minutes during which you can
   go away and ignore the kitchen)

3 large onions
1 tbsp olive oil
2 x 50g tins anchovies, drained
   (reserve the oil)

4 very large potatoes
butter, for greasing
around 450ml double cream (2 small cartons),
   combined with 150ml milk to make 600ml
   total liquid
salt and freshly ground black pepper

Cut the onions in half and then thinly slice into half moons. Heat the oil in a frying or sauté pan (as you want a lot of surface area), for which you have a lid, on a medium to low heat, then add the onions. Add the oil from the anchovy tins too, along with a pinch of salt, and cook for about 20 minutes or so, with the lid on – monitoring the heat and turning down, if necessary – until they are golden brown and soft.

Peel and thinly slice the potatoes lengthways: it's important to slice the potatoes as thinly as possible, and a mandoline is really useful here. If you do use one, please watch your fingers. A sliced thumb tends to ruin your dinner. Otherwise, just use a very sharp knife and slice the potatoes as thinly as you can. Blot the potato slices with kitchen towel to remove some of the starch.

Grease a roasting tin or ovenproof dish with butter, then place a layer of potato slices at the bottom. Season with salt and pepper – be very sparing with the salt as the anchovies are already salty – then top with half of the onions and a few anchovies (we like to place them in diagonal lines). Repeat until all the potatoes are used up: you should have 3 layers of potato slices, 2 layers of onions (as the top layer has no onions) and 3 layers of anchovies (as the final few are placed on the top layer of potatoes). Drizzle over any remaining anchovy tin oil (waste not, want not, etc), then pour over the cream-milk mix and season.

Bake for 45 minutes, or until golden and bubbling. Serve with a green salad with a mustardy French dressing.

That's a Wrap

There is something infinitely joyful about reviving the dishes of one's youth. Central to our late teens was the culinary institution of Fajita Night, beloved of mums everywhere and popular to this day. The instructions are simple: grate Cheddar, open salsa, fry chicken and pepper in oil, add the pre-mixed spice mix, microwave the wraps and ta-da! Dinner.

In our homes, 'fadge' night has progressed from the shouty, grabby affairs of old, to a more sophisticated contemporary (or so we like to think) 'wrap night'. Oh yes. Below are some suggestions for delicious wrap fillings, that take no time to cook or prepare, leaving you to enjoy the company of the friends at your table. The key here is not to overfill your wrap (i.e. don't be that person who tries to stuff a whole crispy duck in your pancake), but go for the whole hog and aim to consume two, if not three, in one sitting.

If you're feeling nice, serve more than one of the suggested filling combinations below. But remember, this is about dinners that require little effort on your part: just one of the fillings below is sure to be a stand-alone crowd-pleaser.

Lime-Marinated Cod Wraps with Red Onion and Tomato

Although written for cod, the marinade can be used on any fish or crustacean so make do with what you can find. The serving sizes below are based on two wraps per person (but of course you could have more…).

Serves 4

Preparation time: 10 minutes, plus 15 minutes marinating
Cooking time: 20 minutes

400g cod fillets
2 tbsp olive oil, plus extra for drizzling
1 tbsp fish sauce
juice of 1 lime

1 tsp sugar
1 red chilli, seeded and thinly sliced into rounds
300g cherry tomatoes
8 tortilla wraps
½ red onion
2 tbsp fresh coriander
100ml natural yoghurt
salt and freshly ground black pepper

Preheat the oven to 180°C/gas 4

Cut the cod (removing any skin first) into chunks and place in a bowl, along with the oil, fish sauce, lime juice, sugar and chilli. Leave to marinate in the fridge for 15 minutes.

Meanwhile, slice the cherry tomatoes in half and place, cut sides up, on a baking tray, drizzle over a little olive oil and season with salt and pepper. Bake for 15 minutes.

About 10 minutes before you are ready to serve, place a large frying pan on a medium heat, and once hot, pour in the fish and marinade. Half poach, half fry the fish until opaque and flaking, turning once, if necessary.

Meanwhile, wrap the tortillas in foil and warm in the oven for a few minutes. Slice the onion and chop the coriander (the stalks finely, the leaves less so), then add to the cooked fish and mix well.

Serve the wraps topped with the quick-baked tomatoes and warm fish salad on top, along with a few teaspoons of yoghurt on each.

Halloumi and Mint Wraps

Where would we be without halloumi? Our vegetarian (and non-veggie) friends rejoice at this wrap option.

Serves 4

Preparation time: 10 minutes
Cooking time: 10 minutes

2 x 225g packets halloumi
15g butter
2 courgettes
drizzle of extra-virgin olive oil
squeeze of lemon juice, plus extra to taste

2 little gem lettuces
50g fresh mint
100ml natural yoghurt
8 tortilla wraps
salt, to taste
jarred Spanish hot peppers,
    to serve (optional)
chilli sauce, to serve (optional)

Preheat the oven to 180°C/gas 4.

Place a large frying pan on a medium heat and slice the halloumi into 5mm-thick slices. Add the butter to the pan and when melted, fry the halloumi in batches until brown on each side.

While the batches of cheese are frying, use a veggie peeler to cut the courgettes into ribbons. Place in a bowl with a drizzle of oil and a squeeze of lemon juice on top; mix lightly together. Set aside.

Chop up the lettuces and mint (minus the stalks) and place in separate serving bowls. Decant the yoghurt into another bowl and add a little salt and lemon juice to taste.

Wrap the tortillas in foil and warm in the oven for a few minutes.

Serve the wraps with the lettuce and courgettes piled on first, followed by the halloumi, mint and a drizzle of yoghurt. Jarred Spanish peppers and chilli sauce are optional, but definitely recommended.

Chorizo and Red Cabbage Wraps

Chorizo is one of those fantastic ingredients that needs little else adding to it. You could add some jarred (pickled) Spanish hot peppers to this if you want some extra zing.

Serves 4

Preparation time: 10 minutes
Cooking time: 10 minutes

2 x 225g chorizo rings
2 carrots
squeeze or two of lemon juice
drizzle of extra virgin olive oil

¼ red cabbage
100ml natural yoghurt
8 tortilla wraps
handful of parsley leaves
salt and freshly ground black pepper
sriracha chilli sauce, to serve (optional)

Preheat the oven to 180°C/gas 4.

Place a frying pan on a medium heat and slice the chorizo slightly diagonally so you have oval-shaped rings, about 5mm thick. Add the chorizo to the pan (no need for oil) and fry until crisp and darker in places. This usually takes about 6 minutes.

Meanwhile, grate the carrots into a bowl, then squeeze over a little lemon juice, add a drizzle of oil and season with salt and pepper. Finely shred the cabbage and place in a separate bowl, ready to serve. Add the yoghurt to another little dish and loosen with a little more lemon juice. Set aside.

Wrap the tortillas in foil and warm in the oven for a few minutes. Chop up the parsley leaves and pop in a bowl. Give the chorizo a quick blast of heat to warm through if it has been ready for a while.

When you are ready to eat, start by layering the cabbage on each wrap, followed by the carrots and chorizo. Finish off with the yoghurt, spooned over, and a scattering of parsley. Chilli sauce is always a welcome addition.

Spicy Bean and Lime Salsa Wraps

This recipe takes a little longer to cook than the previous wraps, but on the plus side, the beans keep well and make a delightful packed lunch the following day… The type of bean doesn't really matter; this would be delicious with chickpeas or borlotti beans.

Serves 4

Preparation time: 10 minutes
Cooking time: 25 minutes

For the spicy beans
1 tbsp olive oil
1 onion
1½ tsp smoked paprika
1 tsp ground coriander
1 tsp cayenne pepper
2 x 400g tins black beans, drained and rinsed
1 x 400g tin chopped tomatoes
20g fresh coriander

For the salsa
200g cherry tomatoes or any ripe tomatoes
½ red onion
lime juice, to taste
extra-virgin olive oil, to taste
salt and freshly ground black pepper

8 tortilla wraps
60g Cheddar
125ml natural yoghurt

Preheat the oven to 180°C/gas 4. For the spicy beans, drizzle the olive oil into a saucepan on a medium heat. Finely chop the onion, add to the pan and soften, then add the spices. Stir for 30 seconds, releasing the aromas, then add the black beans, followed by the tomatoes and ½ tinful of water. Chop up the coriander stalks, reserving the leaves. Add the stalks to the pan, season, then simmer, partially covered, for 15–20 minutes.

Meanwhile, for the salsa, if you're using cherry tomatoes, slice them into pretty little quarters (or chop up larger tomatoes) and thinly slice the onion. Add to a bowl and drizzle over some lime juice and extra-virgin olive oil. Sprinkle over some salt and pepper. Mix, then taste to check the seasoning – it should be nice and zingy and zesty.

Wrap the tortillas in foil and warm in the oven for a few minutes. Grate the Cheddar into a bowl, and decant the yoghurt into another. Roughly chop the reserved coriander leaves. When you are ready to eat, layer the wraps with the spicy beans, Cheddar, yoghurt, salsa and chopped coriander leaves.

DIRTY TUESDAYS

This chapter pays homage to our student days of old. On these eponymous and indeed now infamous 'dirty' Tuesdays, Sophie and friends would cook for themselves, concocting dishes best described as Iceland's equivalents of the bird-in-a-bird-in-a-bird: chicken Kiev on a bed of garlic-laden spaghetti with a side of garlic bread, quadruple cheese mac 'n' cheese with – you guessed it – cheesy garlic bread, and fish-finger-on-a-fish-cake-on-fish-and-chips.

Okay, maybe not that last one – but you get the picture. Whilst we've steered clear of anything too outrageous here (you may well be disappointed at the low profile of the 'battered' food group), this chapter is an unabashed tribute to the unclassy, predominantly beige, but ever so attractive underworld of naughty comfort food. And whilst Kim-Cheese on Toast (page 143) may barely be described as a recipe, we are sure you'll appreciate its inclusion here.

Return of the Mac

Mac and cheese has enjoyed a sublime revival in recent years, now peppering the menus of many a trendy restaurant. Yet, and perhaps because of, its inherent richness, the mac appears to have been relegated to the position of side dish. Here, it is very much the main act, the addition of smoked bacon and cherry tomatoes, cutting through the oozy creaminess, enabling you to eat a bold, heaped plateful of the stuff.

Serves 4 — 6

Preparation time: 15 minutes
Cooking time: 40 minutes

4 rashers streaky bacon
1 tbsp olive oil, plus extra for drizzling
500g macaroni
50g butter, plus extra for greasing
50g plain flour
600ml whole milk
generous grating of nutmeg

1 heaped tsp Colman's or English mustard
1 tbsp Marmite
3 Laughing Cow or Dairylea cheese triangles
60g Cheddar
150g cherry tomatoes
10g grated Parmesan
dried breadcrumbs or crumbled ready salted
    crisps, for sprinkling (optional)
salt and freshly ground black pepper

Preheat the oven to 180°C/gas 4 and butter a large ovenproof pie or roasting dish.

Snip the bacon into little chunks and fry in the oil until nice and crispy. Drain on kitchen towel until you are ready to use it.

Place a large pan of salted water on to boil and when bubbling, add the macaroni. Cook until the pasta is al dente, then pour into a colander and cool under the running cold tap. Drain well, then return to the pan with a drizzle of oil stirred through to prevent the pasta sticking together.

While the bacon and pasta are cooking, melt the butter in a medium-sized, heavy-bottomed saucepan over a medium heat and stir in the flour. Mix vigorously with a wooden spoon or whisk until you have a paste, then begin to drizzle in the milk in stages, stirring quickly or whisking as you go. When all the milk has been incorporated, add the nutmeg, mustard and Marmite. Simmer for a few minutes to thicken, stirring now and then. Add the cheese triangles and mix until melted and incorporated. Turn the heat off. Grate in the Cheddar, then taste the sauce and adjust the seasoning, if necessary.

In the largest pan you've used, combine the pasta, cheese sauce and bacon. Spoon into your buttered dish, then using your thumb, squish in the cherry tomatoes, but don't cover them completely. Top with a grating of Parmesan and a sprinkling of breadcrumbs or crisps, if using. Bake for 20–30 minutes, until the top is golden brown in bits, then serve.

Deluxe Dog

This is not a dignified dinner. It's a messy monster of a sandwich made from quintessential cornershop ingredients. Speedy to shop for, quick to throw together once you're home, and easily scaled up or down, it's ideal for scarfing on the sofa with a few beers and friends.

As with a burger, customise your dog according to your personal likes: extra mustard, chilli sauce, fried onions or – dare we suggest – melted grated cheese.

Serves 4

Preparation time: 15 minutes
Cooking time: 10 minutes

For the pickled cabbage relish
½ small red cabbage
2½ tbsp red wine vinegar
teeny pinch of sugar
salt and freshly ground black pepper

For the mustard beans
1 x 415g tin baked beans
2 tbsp Colman's or English mustard
good squirt of HP or BBQ sauce

For the dogs
8 frankfurters
1 wide (i.e. not skinny) long fresh baguette,
    cut into 4 equal portions (or use 2 ready-
    to-bake baguettes, baked as per the packet
    instructions, then cooled and each cut into
    2 portions)
mayonnaise, for spreading

To finish the beasts
2 spring onions, thinly sliced
sliced pickled jalapeños

Preheat your grill to high.

For the pickled cabbage relish, use a mandoline or a sharp knife to slice the cabbage as thinly as you possibly can without maiming yourself, then chop roughly (so you are left with bite-sized pieces rather than long strands). Place in a bowl with all the other relish ingredients, then give it a good mix and leave to get pickling.

For the mustard beans, add the baked beans to a pan with the mustard and HP sauce and cook gently until thickened slightly, stirring occasionally so the mix doesn't catch.

Meanwhile, for the dogs, place the frankfurters under the grill and cook, turning every so often, until hot and crispy. About 5 minutes before you think they're done, slice the baguette portions in half, leaving a hinge on one side of each portion. Rip out any excess crumb from the middle of either side (you can save this for breadcrumbs), then place the baguette pieces, cut sides up, under the grill to lightly toast, before removing, along with the franks.

Okay. It's time to layer up. For each dog, spread mayonnaise on the bottom half of the baguette, top with 2 franks, spoon over a couple of tablespoons of mustard beans, a few jalapeños, a mound of pickled cabbage, and a sprinkling of spring onions. Have the kitchen towel to hand and get stuck in.

Steak Dip Sandwich

The world seems to be divided into two groups. Lovers of a wet roast, drenched in gravy – and the dry plate brigade, where flavours and trimmings are kept at safe distances on the plate in neat little piles. This dish is definitely for the former camp: a roast sandwich of dreams, moistened by intermittent dipping between bites into a delicious wine sauce. Definitely not date food as gravy on your neck is entirely possible here.

Serves 2

Preparation time: 15 minutes
Cooking time: 15 minutes

For the sauce
2 tbsp olive oil
3 shallots, halved, or 1 medium-small
  onion, quartered
sprig of rosemary
1 garlic clove
250ml red wine
250ml hot beef stock
knob of butter

For the steak sandwiches
1 steak e.g. sirloin or ribeye
2 small fresh baguettes (or use 2 ready-to-
  bake baguettes, baked as per the
  packet instructions)
2 tsp Dijon mustard
2 tbsp mayonnaise
2 handfuls of watercress or rocket
salt and freshly ground black pepper

Preheat the oven to 140°C/gas 1.

First attend to your sauce. Heat the oil in a small saucepan and add the halved shallots and rosemary. Once the shallots have softened and taken on some colour, lower the heat, then thinly slice and add the garlic. Fry for a minute or two, then turn the heat up and add the wine. Reduce by half, then pour in the hot stock. Simmer for 5–10 minutes, then add the knob of butter. Remove from the heat, cover and keep warm.

While your sauce is simmering, prepare the steak sandwiches. Place a griddle pan on a high heat and get it as hot as you can, then fry your steak to taste. We prefer ours rare, so about 2 minutes on each side suffices. Place the fresh baguettes in the oven to warm, along with a pair of ovenproof ramekins for your dipping sauce.

When the steak is cooked, leave it to rest for a few minutes, then cut into bite-sized slices and season well with salt and pepper. Remove the baguettes from the oven, cut open and remove some of the excess crumb from the middles – you want to make room for your filling. Spread each generously with the mustard and mayonnaise and then add the shallots from the sauce, fishing them out with a slotted spoon. Now divide the seasoned steak between the two sandwiches, along with a handful of watercress or rocket.

Decant the now shallot-less sauce into your hot ramekins, removing any hard rosemary stalks, and serve a ramekin of sauce immediately alongside each steak sandwich on a plate. Dip with abandon.

Noodling Around

Let's be clear: instant noodles – whether it's a packet of BBQ Super Noodles or a fancy(er) Tom Yum flavour with a little sachet of dried shrimps enclosed – are basically the opposite of a health food, and not something that you should eat too regularly, tempting though it may be to do so. But what they lack in superfood status, they more than make up for by being a) delicious b) quick c) readily available in even the most spartan, miserably stocked of cornershops d) cheap e) easy to dress up. So throw away the packet of (fiendishly more-ish, probably 98% MSG) flavouring and get creative: with just a few select additions, a somewhat seedy snack can become a nourishing meal.

Five Ways with Instant Ramen

Poor Man's Pad Thai

Want that takeaway fix but can't afford it? This cheapo version of pad Thai has similar (though obviously less complex) flavours, and costs pennies. Don't skimp on the lime though, as it really needs it.

Preparation time: 3 minutes
Cooking time: 7 minutes

For the sauce
2½ tsp tomato ketchup
1½ tsp soy sauce
merest splash of fish sauce
juice of ¼ lime
tiny pinch of dried chilli flakes
1 tsp peanut butter

For the noodles
1 packet (around 80–90g) instant ramen
  noodles
220ml boiling water
1 egg

To serve
crushed salted peanuts
1 spring onion, thinly sliced
lime wedge

Mix all the sauce ingredients together in a small saucepan and heat gently. Add the noodles to the sauce, cook the noodle brick for a couple of minutes on each side, then add the boiling water. Turn the heat up and baste the noodles with the sauce until they begin to relax and loosen up. Continue stirring until almost all of the liquid is absorbed. Crack in the egg and use a fork to break it up. Stir into the noodles so it scrambles, and cook until done and the liquid is all absorbed. Serve scattered with salted peanuts, spring onion, and a squeeze of lime.

Spamen, or Spam Ramen

The ultimate marriage of cornershop convenience foods. If spam seems one step away from an All Day Breakfast in a tin and therefore too much for you to countenance, you could substitute hot dogs, sliced into slim diagonal wedges. Firm tofu is a good and, dare we say, rather elegant vegetarian alternative. A couple of spring onions can stand in place if you can't find a leek

Preparation time: 5 minutes,
  plus 15 minutes marinating time
Cooking time: 10 minutes

½ red chilli
½ leek
½ garlic clove
1 ½ tbsp soy sauce
1.5cm piece of ginger, peeled and grated
1 tsp sesame oil

1 x 200g tin spam
½ chicken stock cube or jelly stock pot
620ml boiling water
1 packet (around 80–90g) instant
  ramen noodles
½ tsp fish sauce
1 x 6-minute Boiled Egg (see Eggcetera on
  page 135), cooled slightly, then peeled and
  halved, to serve
DIY Garlic Chilli Oil (see page 61), to serve

Seed and thinly slice the chilli, thinly slice the leek and mince or crush the garlic. Combine the chilli, garlic, 1 tablespoon of the soy sauce and the sesame oil in a dish. Remove the spam from its tin (follow the instructions on the side, or, if you're anything like us, you may end up frantically beating the tin with a rolling pin to try and coax the meat out). Cut off three 1cm-thick slices of spam (keep the rest in the fridge for later), add to the chilli mix and turn to coat all over, then leave to marinate for 15 minutes. Place a frying pan on medium heat and fry the spam slices in the marinade until crisp and browned on both sides.

Meanwhile, add the chicken stock cube and boiling water to a small-ish saucepan along with the noodles, and cook on a medium to high heat. When the noodles begin to collapse out of their block form, add the sliced leek and grated ginger. Cook until the noodles are fully done and the stock has reduced a little – a few minutes. Season with the remaining soy sauce and the fish sauce. Add to a bowl and top with the crispy spam, the halved egg, and some garlic chilli oil.

Breakfast-style

Marmite on toast in noodle form.

Cooking time: 10 minutes max

10g butter
1 tsp Marmite
1 packet (around 80–90g) instant
 ramen noodles
220ml boiling water
1 x 6-minute Boiled Egg (see Eggcetera
 opposite), cooled slightly, then peeled and
 sliced
salt and freshly ground black pepper

Melt the butter and Marmite in a small saucepan on a low heat. Add the noodles and cook for 30 seconds, then flip the noodle brick over. Add the boiling water, turn the heat up, and baste the noodles until they begin to relax and loosen up. Continue stirring until all the liquid is absorbed. Serve with the sliced boiled egg on top, seasoned with salt and pepper.

English Cacio e Pepe

Thanks and credit to David Chang for bringing this genius combo into our lives.

Cooking time: 10 minutes max

10g butter
40g grated Cheddar (you could use
 Parmesan too)
240ml boiling water
1 packet (around 80–90g) instant
 ramen noodles
freshly ground black pepper, to taste

Melt the butter in a small saucepan on a low heat. Turn the heat up, add the cheese, some black pepper and the boiling water and whisk furiously until the cheese dissolves into the sauce. Add the noodles and cook for 30 seconds, then flip the noodle brick over. Turn the heat up still further, and baste the noodles until they begin to relax and loosen up. Continue stirring until all the liquid is absorbed. Serve with a twist more black pepper.

Greens

A simple noodle broth to soothe the soul.

Preparation time: 6 minutes
Cooking time: 8 minutes

½ garlic clove
2cm piece of ginger, peeled
1 tsp groundnut or vegetable oil
2 bok choy, or a very large handful of spring
   greens/cabbage, shredded
1 packet (around 80–90g) instant
   ramen noodles
½ vegetable stock cube or jelly stock pot

620ml boiling water
soy sauce, to taste
fish sauce, to taste

To serve
2cm piece of red chilli, seeded
   and thinly sliced
1 spring onion, thinly sliced
DIY Garlic Chilli Oil (see page 61) (optional)
1 x 6-minute Boiled Egg (see below), cooled
   slightly, then peeled and cut in half

Finely chop the garlic and ginger and cook in the oil in a small-ish saucepan for a couple of minutes, until beginning to soften. Slice the bok choy or greens into quarters, then add to the pan, along with the noodles. Add the stock cube and boiling water. Put the lid on and cook until the noodles are done, stirring once or twice. Add the soy sauce and fish sauce to the broth to taste. Serve topped with red chilli, spring onion, chilli oil and the halved egg.

Eggcetera

Everyone has their own perfect egg making methods — this is ours.

Fill a pan (large enough for however many eggs you're cooking) three-quarters full with boiled water fresh from the kettle. Turn on the heat, and as soon as the water begins to boil (no, a faint-hearted simmer does not count), add your egg(s) and set your stopwatch. (The temperature should lower after adding the egg(s), but you may want to decrease the temperature a little so it's not at a rollicking boil.) As soon as the allotted time is up, remove the pan from the heat and run under loads of cold water. Leave the egg(s) to cool for a couple of minutes, then peel.

6 minutes: just about semi-set white, not fully liquid but very oozy yolk.

6½ minutes: firmer, with a set white, and a yolk that has a smidgen of runniness.

Croque-Person a Cheval

Ah, the Croque Monsieur: our go-to hangover brunch in Paris when a croissant is in no conceivable way going to cut the mustard. It is the closest you can get to the curative Full English on the continent after an ill-advised night out.

In spite of the cold hard fact that it is essentially cheese on toast, a Croque Monsieur (or Madame) can feel surprisingly sophisticated when eaten in the context of a Parisian cafe terrace. Back at home, it is a cosy meal for two (the spare après-sandwich can either be shared or fought over). Serve with a side salad of lettuce and tomato with a mustardy French dressing.

Makes 3 sandwiches

Preparation time: 25 minutes
Cooking time: 6–8 minutes

15g butter, plus extra for spreading and frying
15g plain flour
splash of dry white wine
250ml milk
grating of nutmeg
50g mature Cheddar or Emmenthal
6 slices of bread of your choice

50g young spinach leaves, rinsed
1 ripe avocado
juice of ½ lemon (about 2 tsp)
sprinkling of dried chilli flakes or a few drops
   of chilli sauce
6 slices of ham
1 tbsp olive oil
3 eggs
salt and freshly ground black pepper

Melt the butter in a heavy-bottomed saucepan on a medium heat and add the flour. Mix with a wooden spoon until you have a paste, and continue stirring for a couple of minutes to cook the flour without browning it. Add the wine, followed by the milk, ever so gradually, all the while stirring. Make sure the heat is high enough (although not too high) otherwise the sauce won't thicken, and bring to a fast simmer. Cook for about 5 minutes, stirring regularly. Use a hand whisk or hand-held stick blender to disperse any lumps. Take off the heat, season with the nutmeg and salt and pepper, then grate in the cheese and stir some more.

Meanwhile, preheat your grill to high. Lightly toast the bread on both sides. Butter one side of 3 of the slices, and place on a baking tray, buttered-side down. Top each with the spinach leaves.

Remove the stone from the avocado and scoop out the flesh into a bowl. Sprinkle over some salt, the lemon juice and chilli flakes. Mash and mix well, then drop dollops of the mixture on top of the spinach leaves. Top each sandwich half with 2 slices of ham, slicing and overlapping where necessary to keep it all in.

Spoon over a thin layer of cheese sauce (saving plenty for the topping) and close off each sandwich with a piece of toast. Neatly pour over the remaining cheese sauce, and then place under the grill for 6–8 minutes. Keep an eye on them: they are ready when the topping is bubbling a little and has gone golden brown in parts.

While the sandwiches are grilling, heat a knob of butter and the oil in a frying pan. Crack in the eggs and fry on a fairly high heat until cooked to your liking.

Top each croque-person with a fried egg and serve immediately.

Meatball Sub

Meatballs aren't just the preserve of pasta; you can have them in a sandwich. If you want extra crunch, some carrot ribbons would work well in this too.

Serves 2

Preparation time: 15 minutes
Cooking time: 30 minutes

squeeze of tomato ketchup
salt and freshly ground black pepper

For the tomato dipping sauce
2 tbsp olive oil
1 garlic clove, sliced
1 x 400g carton or jar passata or
  1 x 400g tin chopped tomatoes
pinch of dried oregano
1 tsp sugar
dash of Worcestershire sauce

For the meatball sub
1 tbsp olive oil
6–8 meatballs
1 fresh baguette or 2
  ready-to-bake baguettes
½ red onion
30g Cheddar
handful of basil leaves

Preheat the oven to 160°C/gas 3.

First attend to your tomato dipping sauce, as this needs to be cooked fairly slowly. Heat the oil in a pan on a low heat and add the garlic. Cook for a minute and the moment you see the garlic threatening to change colour, add the passata or tomatoes, followed by the oregano, sugar, Worcestershire sauce, ketchup and seasoning. Leave this to simmer happily, uncovered, for 10–15 minutes while you cook the meatballs.

For the meatball sub, place a frying pan on a medium heat and add the oil, then fry the meatballs for about 8–10 minutes until cooked through. (You could also bake them in the oven.)

Towards the end of the meatball cooking time, place the fresh baguette in the oven to warm, along with a pair of ovenproof ramekins for the dipping sauce. (If you're using ready-to-bake baguettes, you'll need to increase the oven temperature and bake them according to the packet instructions.)

Thinly slice the red onion, along with the cheese. Taste the tomato sauce and adjust the seasoning, if necessary.

Remove the baguettes from the oven and slice open. You shouldn't need to butter or spread mayonnaise on the bread as your dipping sauce will provide all the moisture you need.

Layer the base of each baguette with the basil leaves, followed by the cheese slices and the onion. Slice the meatballs in half and share between each baguette, cut-sides down. Cut the sandwiches in half, then place each on a plate.

Carefully remove the warmed ramekins from the oven and pop on to the sandwich plates. Ladle in some tomato dipping sauce. Serve immediately.

London Tartiflette

There's no real way to justify the gluttonous nature of this recipe. It is traditionally enjoyed in the French mountains after a respectable day's skiing where you will have burned somewhere in the region of 2000 calories. Well, if you're anything like us, you count blow-drying your hair as exercise. Oh dear. But you know... working 5+ days a week is pretty hard. So just enjoy this version with your pals, alongside a little gem lettuce salad with a mustardy French dressing to cut through the naughtiness: you've earned it. Oh and did we also mention that it is gluten-free? Practically wipes the slate clean (although you may want to mop up some of that cheesy goodness with a baguette...).

We use Brie and/or Camembert in our convenience shop version, as Reblochon is difficult if not impossible to come by locally. Purists, look away now.

Serves 4 hungry people

Preparation time: 10 minutes
Cooking time: 40 minutes

1kg waxy potatoes
550ml whole milk
generous grating of nutmeg
200ml double cream

knob of butter, plus extra for greasing
1 onion
200g smoked streaky bacon rashers
2 garlic cloves, crushed
300g Brie or Camembert
salt and freshly ground black pepper

Preheat the oven to 180°C/gas 4. Grease a large ovenproof pie dish with butter.

Peel the potatoes and slice into thin rounds. Place in a large pan and cover with the milk. Add a pinch of salt and pepper and the nutmeg, and simmer on a low heat for about 15–20 minutes until they are just cooked, stirring occasionally to make sure no slices get stuck to the bottom. Stir in the cream, then turn the heat off.

While the potatoes are cooking, melt the knob of butter in a frying pan on a medium heat. Thinly slice the onion and add to the pan. Snip the bacon rashers into pieces while the onion gets a cooking head start, then add to the same frying pan with the garlic. Cook for a further few minutes, then remove from the heat and set aside.

When the potatoes are tender and you have added the cream, gently stir in the cooked onion, bacon and garlic. Pour the potato mix into the greased pie dish, spreading evenly. Finally, cut the cheese into slices and slot in-between the top lateral potato slices.

Bake for 20 minutes until the cheese is golden and the top potatoes are crispy in bits. Serve immediately.

Kim-Cheese on Toast

You don't have to make your own kimchi: shop-bought kimchi is brilliant and readily available at Asian shops. If that's not an option, you can always buy it online or you could use sauerkraut, or pickled red cabbage, with a dribble of chilli sauce squeezed over the top, instead.

Makes 1

Preparation time: 3 minutes (basically just cheese grating)
Cooking time: 6–8 minutes (or longer if using a ready-to-bake baguette)

1 slice of bread (or a split ready-to-bake baguette works a treat, as does a pitta bread)

½ garlic clove
kimchi — enough to cover surface of said bread
grated sharp Cheddar — enough to cover surface of kimchi covering surface of bread

Preheat your grill to high.

Lightly toast the bread on both sides. If using a ready-to-bake baguette, bake in a preheated oven according to the package instructions. If using a pitta bread, toast, then split and use both halves.

Rub the top/cut surface of the toasted bread/baguette/pitta with the cut side of garlic, and then top with a thin layer of kimchi. Cover with a generous layer of grated Cheddar. Toast under the grill until the cheese is bubbling and crusty. Repeat until supplies are depleted or fullness is achieved.

Frankfurter Fried Rice

You can make this spicier by replacing the sweet chilli with a hotter chilli sauce, or adding half a sliced (seeded) red chilli, along with the spring onions and garlic. The greens and peas add a small but welcome element of freshness, but aren't 100% necessary. If you're lucky enough to have a jar of kimchi in the fridge, then chop some up and add it in too.

Serves 2 generously as dinner

Preparation time: 15 minutes
Cooking time (including standing time):
   35 minutes

150g frozen peas
150g long-grain white rice
300ml water
6 spring onions

1 garlic clove
handful of cabbage leaves or greens
4 frankfurters
2 eggs
around 3 tbsp soy sauce
small splash of sesame oil
splash of sweet chilli sauce
1 tbsp vegetable or groundnut oil

Measure out the peas and leave them to thaw a bit. Rinse the rice in a colander, then add to a small saucepan with a lid and cover with the water. Bring to the boil, then turn down the heat to low, put on the lid and cook for around 20 minutes, until all the water has been absorbed. When the rice is done, turn off the heat and leave it to stand for 5 minutes, with the lid still on.

Meanwhile, get everything ready for your wok/frying pan. Thinly slice the spring onions, finely chop the garlic and slice the cabbage roughly. Slice the frankfurters into 1cm pieces. Beat the eggs in a bowl, and have the soy sauce, sesame oil and sweet chilli sauce to hand.

Put your wok or large frying pan on a high (but not raging) heat. When it is hot (hold your hand over it if you want to make sure), add the vegetable oil. When the oil is hot, add the frankfurters. Stir-fry for 2 – 3 minutes, or until brown and turning a little crisp around the edges. Add the spring onions, garlic and cabbage and stir-fry for a couple more minutes, then add the peas and stir-fry until fully done (try one to check).

Add the beaten eggs and stir repeatedly and quickly so they scramble. Add the soy sauce, sesame oil and chilli sauce and stir, then add the cooked rice. Stir, stir, stir. Continue cooking for a few more minutes – the rice should be piping hot. Serve immediately.

THE UNPLANNED DINNER PARTY

Sometimes – okay, let's be honest, often – despite our best intentions, we find ourselves underprepared for people coming for dinner. You know the score: whether it's old friends you've finally managed to pin down, or the couple who live down the road who had you round five months ago, it's been in the diary for weeks.

Of course, you've forgotten about it. Then remembered it. Stressed about it and considered rearranging. Forgotten about it again; then realised it's too late. Before you know it, it's the night before and you're stuck at the office or at some work do you put in your work Outlook calendar but not your personal diary (or maybe it's even the weekend, but you've frittered it away doing chores): either way, there is now no way you can visit the shops you'd planned to blitz in advance (the butcher, the special cheese place, the bakery…) to ensure calm competency on the day, let alone do a rudimentary clean of your frankly squalid bathroom.

The reality is that you're going to get home at 6.30pm at the earliest – factor in swinging by the shop, and 7pm is more likely (and that's if you act like you're in Supermarket Sweep). What you need is something cooking by 7.30pm that will require little attention henceforth. Besides the obligatory panic-shop of houmous, olives, kettle crisps and enough fizzy wine to befuddle your guests, this chapter outlines some delicious recipes you can cook for midweek or last minute DPs.

For the majority, we've aimed for little prep relative to cooking time (after all, you are meant to talk to your guests) and enjoyment. Those recipes that do require more involvement compensate by being made from ingredients that you can pick up with ease (i.e. no panicked dash to the only supermarket that sells palatable meat).

Spicy Fish Stew with Rice and Golden Plantain

Plantain, a relative of the banana, acts as a delicious mouth coolant in this recipe, much as lassi or yoghurt would in Indian cooking. We serve our plantain sliced and fried, which caramelises the flesh.

This spicy tomato sauce is adaptable and can be used with any fish you wish. If your local mini supermarket serves tuna steaks, for example (ethically sourced of course), then pounce on them and simply fry separately in oil and serve just cooked with the sauce spooned on top.

Serves 4

Preparation time: 10 minutes
Cooking time: 30 minutes

1–2 tbsp olive oil
4 salmon fillets, skin on
juice of 1 lime
1 onion
2 garlic cloves
2 x 400g tins chopped tomatoes
1 tbsp tomato purée
1 tsp freshly ground black pepper

1 tsp sugar
½ tsp dried thyme
2 Scotch bonnet chillies (removed at the end of cooking) or 1 red chilli, seeded and finely chopped
150g long-grain rice
15g butter
2 ripe plantains, peeled and sliced into rounds
salt, to taste

Heat 1 tablespoon of the oil in a large pan (big enough to accommodate all the pieces of fish) on a medium to high heat, then flash-fry the salmon for a few minutes, skin side down, until you see some colour. Remove the fish to a plate and squeeze a little lime juice over, then set to one side and keep warm. Turn the heat down to low.

Finely chop the onion and add to the pan you cooked the fish in with the remaining oil, if needed. Leave the onion to soften, while you slice the garlic. When the onion is going translucent and a little brown in bits, add the garlic and cook for about a minute, before pouring over the tomatoes. Stir in the tomato purée and then add the black pepper, sugar, thyme and a generous amount of salt. Add the chillies and leave to reduce and simmer, uncovered, for 20 minutes.

Once your sauce is on, cook the rice according to the packet instructions, then drain (if necessary).

About 5 minutes before you are ready to serve, add the butter to a frying pan and add the plantain slices. Fry until golden and crispy on the outside.

Return the salmon to the pan with the tomato sauce to finish cooking through for a few minutes, then squeeze over some more lime juice.

Serve the fish fillets and tomato sauce with the rice and plantain on warmed plates, discarding the Scotch bonnet chillies, if using.

Spicy Braised Fennel, Served with Sausages

There is no earthly reason why sausages can't make an elegant meal. One of the best dinner parties we've ever attended was thrown by Lucy Buglass of Aberdeenshire and consisted of commendable bangers and mash. Here we are pairing the sausages with fennel – another match made in heaven.

Serves 4

Preparation time: 20 minutes
Cooking time: 45 minutes

8–12 Cumberland sausages
3 fennel bulbs
2 onions
2 tbsp extra-virgin olive oil

200ml dry white wine (plus extra, if needed)
6 ripe tomatoes or 1 x 400g tin chopped tomatoes
1 red chilli, seeded
2 bay leaves
1 tsp fennel seeds
salt and freshly ground black pepper

Preheat the oven to 180°C/gas 4.

Put the sausages in a roasting tin and bake for 30 minutes, turning occasionally.

Meanwhile, trim and chop each fennel bulb in half, then slice each half into 3 sections. Cut the onions into quarters. Add the fennel and onions to a pan with the oil, and cook on a medium heat until they take on some colour. (If you're using fresh, not tinned tomatoes, now put the kettle on.)

Add the white wine to the pan, mix well, then leave the fennel and onions to braise, stirring occasionally, until the wine has reduced by half. This usually takes around 5 – 10 minutes.

While the fennel and onions are cooking in the wine, pop the fresh tomatoes in a heatproof bowl and cover with boiling water. After a minute, fish out the tomatoes, cool under the tap and carefully peel off the skins (if you are pressed for time, you can skip this stage and leave the skins on). Finely chop the fresh tomatoes, along with the red chilli, and add to the pan (if you are using tinned tomatoes, add them now), together with the bay leaves, fennel seeds and a sprinkling of salt and pepper.

Cover the pan with a lid and turn down the heat, then leave the fennel and onions to simmer and stew while the sausages finish cooking, but check on the pan regularly and add a little hot water or extra wine, if needed.

When everything is cooked through, spoon the spicy fennel and onions, which should be nice and soft, on to warmed plates, then top with the sausages, sliced open lengthways. Enjoy.

Spinach and Artichoke Orzo Bake

This is a combination of two delicious things that you should indulge in very rarely and that taste especially good after one too many drinks (ideal for a dinner party, then): the pasta bake and the spinach artichoke dip. If you can't find orzo, use another small type of pasta.

Serves 4 — 6, depending on levels of hunger/greed

Preparation time: 15 minutes
Cooking time: 45 minutes

1 large onion.
4 garlic cloves
2 jalapeños or 1 small (but not fiendishly tiny) green chilli
2 x 290g jars artichoke hearts in oil (or equivalent weight of tinned artichoke hearts)

3 tbsp olive oil
400g young or baby spinach, rinsed
6 heaped tbsp crème fraîche or natural yoghurt
75g grated Cheddar
100g grated Parmesan
500g orzo
2 x 125g packets mozzarella balls, drained
salt and freshly ground black pepper

Preheat the oven to 200°C/gas 6.

Finely chop the onion and garlic. Seed and chop the jalapeños. Drain the artichokes and cut each one in half, then cut each half into 3. Heat the oil in a deep, cast–iron ovenproof pan, add the onion and garlic and cook for 10–12 minutes. Add the jalapeños and artichokes and cook for a further 5 minutes or so. Add the spinach and put the lid on the pan. Cook until it wilts down. (Put a pan of water on to boil for the orzo at this point.)

Add the crème fraîche to the pan and mix together. Add the Cheddar and 75g of the Parmesan and mix. When the cheese has melted, season, taste and add more salt and pepper as required.

Cook the orzo in the pan of boiling water for just under the recommended time – around 7–8 minutes. While you're waiting, chop the mozzarella into small cubes.

Drain the orzo, reserving some of the cooking water. Add the orzo to the spinach sauce and mix together. If it looks like it needs a bit more moisture, add some of the reserved cooking water.

Give it all a good mix, taste to check the seasoning, then add the mozzarella cubes and remaining Parmesan to the top and bake for 15 minutes.

If you want a crusty top, finish under a hot grill for about 10 minutes, or until crunchy and golden brown.

Chorizo on White Beans

Arguably a posh version of the ubiquitous Heinz beans and sausages, this simple yet sophisticated meal should be served alongside a green salad, some crusty bread and copious amounts of Sancerre. Carrying the beans home from the cornershop will also give your arms a workout. We don't serve it with a huge amount of chorizo as it is a strong sausage. But if you and your guests are fans, just up the quantity.

Serves 4

Preparation time: 5 minutes
Cooking time: 25 minutes

3 tbsp olive oil
3 garlic cloves, sliced
250ml dry white wine

5 x 400g tins butter beans or cannellini beans
pinch of dried thyme, plus a little extra
600–800ml hot chicken stock, as needed
1 x 225g chorizo ring
salt and freshly ground black pepper

Heat the oil in a heavy-bottomed casserole pot on a medium heat, then add the garlic. After a minute or two, pour in the wine and burn off the alcohol.

Drain and rinse the beans. Add to the casserole pot, along with a pinch of thyme and approximately 600ml of the hot stock. Bring to the boil, then simmer fast, uncovered, for 25 minutes, stirring frequently and topping up with stock as necessary: the idea is to serve the beans quite saucy.

While the beans are cooking, slice the chorizo. About 5 minutes before you are ready to serve, put a non stick frying pan on a medium to high heat and fry the chorizo with a little extra thyme, until the chorizo is crispy and a tiny bit charred in parts. Taste the beans, adding salt and pepper, as necessary. Remove the chorizo from the heat and leave to one side while you ladle the beans on to 4 plates. Arrange the cooked chorizo on top, taking care to drizzle over some of the naughty but delicious crimson oil from the frying pan. Serve.

Beanie Fish Bake with Salsa Verde

A take on the ubiquitous fish pie with added pulses and a paradoxically 1970s yet sophisticated sauce. Good for the weeknight dinner party in that while the bake cooks, you can attend to your guests/slob out eating pistachios.

Serves 3 — 4

Preparation time: 25 minutes
Cooking time: 1 hour

For the salsa verde
2 garlic cloves
2 anchovies
30g fresh mint, leaves picked
30g fresh basil, leaves picked
1 tbsp gherkins or cornichons
1 tbsp capers
2 tbsp red wine vinegar
6 tbsp extra-virgin olive oil

For the bake
15g butter, plus extra for greasing
15g plain flour
200ml milk
1 tsp Dijon mustard
200ml double cream
1 x 400g tin butter beans
500g skinless, boneless white fish fillets
500g potatoes
grating of Parmesan

Preheat the oven to 180°C/gas 4.

For the bake, melt the butter in a milk pan (or a small, heavy-bottomed pan) on a medium heat and then sprinkle in the flour, stirring with a wooden spoon as you go. When incorporated into a paste, begin to trickle the milk in, little by little, adding more as it becomes incorporated, and continually stirring or whisking to prevent lumps. When you have finished adding the milk, leave to simmer for a few minutes, stirring occasionally to prevent the sauce sticking, before taking off the heat. Cool slightly, then add the mustard and cream.

Drain and rinse the butter beans and cut the fish into chunks. Peel the potatoes and slice into thin rounds (a mandoline would be useful here).

Grease a pie dish with extra butter and then layer the potatoes, butter beans and fish as you wish, ending with an artful layer of potatoes for the aesthetes among you. Pour over your white

sauce, using the back of a spoon to spread it evenly over the top, and then finish with a grating of Parmesan.

Bake for 1 hour. At the end, check the potatoes are cooked by slotting a knife into them: they should be soft. Turn the oven up and give the lot a quick blast to finish off, if need be.

While the dish is baking, attend to the salsa verde. Crush the garlic cloves and pound or mash the anchovies into a paste. Chop the herbs finely, along with the gherkins and capers. Mix together in a bowl, then add the red wine vinegar and oil and mix again.

When you're ready, serve portions of the bake with a generous tablespoon or two of the salsa verde spooned on top.

Pasta e Fagioli

A comforting Italian classic – and a cornershop classic too. Buy the nicest brand of beans you can. Serve with extra Parmesan for grating, good bread for mopping and a simple salad to fulfill the something green quota.

Serves 4 — 6

Preparation time: 15 minutes
Cooking time: 50 minutes

2 red onions
2 sticks celery
1 large carrot
4 garlic cloves
5 tbsp extra-virgin olive oil,
   plus extra to serve
large sprig of rosemary (or use ½ tsp dried)
1 bay leaf

200g tinned plum tomatoes
3 x 400g tins borlotti beans, drained
   and rinsed
hard end of your Parmesan, chopped off
   (about 2.5cm wide)
1.5 litres hot stock (made with 2 tbsp
   bouillon powder)
300g macaroni or other small pasta
salt and freshly ground black pepper
grated Parmesan, to serve

Finely dice the onions, celery and carrot, and chop the garlic – keep all the chopped veg separate on your board.

Add the measured oil to a pan and when warm, add the onions and garlic. Cook for a couple of minutes on a medium to low heat, then add the celery, carrot, rosemary and bay leaf. Cook for 10–15 minutes, stirring occasionally, until soft.

Drain the plum tomatoes into a bowl and roughly chop them, removing any tough stalk tops. Add to the pan and cook for 3 minutes. Add two tins of the drained beans, the Parmesan end, and the hot stock. Cook for 20 minutes, with the lid off.

While the bean mix is bubbling away, put a separate large pan of salted water on to boil for the pasta. Cook the pasta for just under its recommended cooking time, so it's still slightly underdone, then drain.

Remove any hard rosemary stalks, the bay leaf and Parmesan rind from your bean mix, then, using a hand-held stick blender, purée the mixture slightly, (you just want to do this a bit, to thicken it). Cook for a further 10 minutes.

Add the additional tin of drained beans and the cooked pasta and season to taste with salt and pepper. Add a splash of water if you think it needs it. Cook for a further 3 minutes, then remove from the heat and leave to cool for a minute or two before serving, with a drizzle of oil and plenty of Parmesan on the table.

Chilli Roast Chicken Tray

Sadly, no cornershops we've ever visited have sold a free-range chicken, so this is definitely a mini supermaket recipe. Spatchcocking the chicken saves on the roasting time and suggests to your guests that you possess hitherto unknown butchery skills. We cook the potatoes from raw – rather than crisping they soak up all the delicious juices beautifully. Do buy the smallest ones you can find: the ideal is what local mini supermarkets call 'miniature potatoes'.

Making the marinade is the only faff – if you're pressed for time, we'd give it a miss. Just buy a 90g jar of harissa (available pretty much everywhere now) and doctor it with additional olive oil, lemon juice and some ground cumin, until you have a thinner mixture with an even balance of flavours. Once the bird's in the oven, you can sit back and relax/frantically clean your bathroom/pour nuts into decorative bowls.

Serves 4

Preparation time: 35 minutes
Cooking time: 1 hour

1 medium chicken (around 1.3–1.5kg)

For the chilli pepper marinade
3 red peppers
5 red chillies
6 garlic cloves
½ tsp cumin seeds
2 tbsp olive oil
juice of ½ lemon
couple of generous pinches of salt

For the potatoes
1kg new, baby or 'miniature' potatoes (or
  equivalent weight in large potatoes)
3 red onions (or 4 if small)
good glug or two of olive oil
good hefty sprinkle of salt
375g baby plum or cherry tomatoes

For the chilli mayo
3 tbsp mayonnaise
4 tbsp chilli pepper marinade (see above)

Preheat the oven to 220°C/gas 7.

For the marinade, cook the peppers and chillies over the bare flames of your gas hob. Don't have the heat too high – you want to char, not decimate them. A pair of tongs is handy for frequent turning – 10 minutes should do the job. If you have an electric hob, cook them under a preheated hot grill instead until they blister. When done, remove to a baking tray and leave to cool.

Put a small saucepan on a high heat. Add the whole garlic cloves (skin still on) and cook for 3–4 minutes. Turn the heat down when you can smell and see that the skins are charring. At this point, add the cumin seeds to the pan. Cook for around a minute (until just starting to colour).

The peppers and chillies should be cool enough to handle now. Put on clean rubber gloves (those disposable ones you get with hair dye are ideal). Peel and seed – it's messy work, so stand near the sink as you'll need to rinse your hands. Don't worry about rogue charred bits or skin that won't come off. Add the flesh to a food processer or use a hand-held blender (if the latter, you may need to process in batches), along with the garlic cloves, squeezed out of their skins, and cumin seeds. Blitz for a minute, then add the oil, lemon juice and salt. Blitz again.

To spatchcock your chicken, turn it breast side down, so the legs are pointing towards you. Using very, very sharp kitchen scissors, cut down either side of the backbone, right up to the end. Employ your sharpest knife if your scissors don't quite cut it. Discard the backbone. Turn back, breast-side up, and squash down with the palms of your hands to flatten. Et voilà. Add 5 tablespoons of the marinade (if using doctored harissa – see intro opposite – use half of your mixture) to a bowl and massage into the chicken. (Use any leftovers as a marinade for veg before you roast them or just refrigirate and use within 2 days). Leave to sit while you do the veg.

For the potatoes, the smallest new potatoes can be left as are; large potatoes should be cut into halves, quarters or small, short chunks. Whatever the potato variety, they should be no wider than 3cm. Cut the onions in half, then into rough, short chunks.

Add the potatoes and onions to a large, deep roasting tin, season with some of the oil and a sprinkling of salt, then push away from the middle, and lay the flattened chicken in the cleared space. Add a bit more oil and salt to the chicken skin before putting in the oven.

When it's been in the oven for 25 minutes, give the potatoes a shuffle and add the tomatoes, then reduce the temperature to 200°C/gas 6. Cook for a further 20–25 minutes. Check that chicken is done by piercing the thickest part of the breast – the juices should run clear.

For the chilli mayo, mix the mayonnaise and marinade together in a small bowl.

Serve the roast chicken and veg with the chilli mayo and a green salad, plus lots of bread for mopping up all the delicious cooking juices.

Cornershop Koshari

Koshari is an Egyptian dish, traditionally vegetarian, made from rice, lentils and pasta, topped with a tomato sauce. All these ingredients should be available from even the most miserably depleted of shops but we've taken some liberties here and simplified our version, swapping the lentils for tinned chickpeas, to save on time (and washing up one more pan…).

It's still not the quickest of recipes in this book (it may even be the longest…), but it is impressive, so it's a great one to make when you have people round, especially if you have a helper on hand to be your sous chef. The yoghurt is in no way traditional but tastes really good.

Serves 4 — 6

Preparation time: 30 minutes
Cooking time: 45 minutes—1 hour

For the Koshari
240g basmati rice
2 tbsp olive oil
3 medium-large onions, halved and sliced
pinch of salt
40g spaghetti, snapped into short little bits
1 tsp groundnut oil or other neutral oil
1 x 400g tin chickpeas, drained and rinsed
480ml boiling water
100g small pasta, like macaroni
20g butter, in small chunks
handful of parsley, leaves picked

For the tomato sauce
2 tbsp olive oil
15g butter
6 garlic cloves, sliced
¾ tsp ground cinnamon
2 x 400g tins plum tomatoes
tiniest pinch of dried chilli flakes
salt and freshly ground black pepper

For the yoghurt sauce
3 heaped tbsp Greek-style natural yoghurt
½ garlic clove, crushed or finely grated
squeeze of lemon juice
sea salt, to taste

First things first, start the koshari: rinse the rice in cold water to remove excess starch, then leave to sit in a bowl of warm water for 20 minutes while you get everything else ready.

Start making the tomato sauce. Add the oil and butter to a pan on a medium heat. When melted, add the garlic and fry for a couple of minutes – as soon as the garlic starts to colour, add the cinnamon and leave to cook for a minute, before adding the tomatoes, crushing them through your hand as you pour them into the pan (or you could use a masher to help break them down once they are in the pan). Add the chilli flakes and season with salt and pepper, then turn the heat down and leave to simmer, uncovered, for around 15 – 20 minutes.

Continue with the koshari. Add the olive oil to another pan – use one for which you have a lid, as you will cook the rice in this later. Put on a medium heat, then add the onions and a pinch of salt. Fry until brown and starting to turn a little bit crisp round the edges. Don't be tempted to try and rush this bit by turning up the heat – it doesn't work (we've tried…).

When the onions have reached the desired cooked-ness, remove from the pan and put on a plate to the side. Heat the same pan again and when hot, add the spaghetti strands. These will go crisp pretty quickly so keep the pan moving, and then remove them to the onion plate when they are brown, crisp and toasted (taste one to check if you're unsure they're cooked through).

Reduce the heat under the tomato sauce or take it off the hob if it looks like it is drying out too much; keep it warm.

Boil a full kettle of water for the rice. Using the same pan that contained the onions/pasta, add the groundnut oil and when hot, add the drained rice and the chickpeas. Cook for a couple of minutes, giving it all a good mix so that everything gets coated. Add the measured boiling water (from the kettle), turn up the heat and bring to the boil, then put a lid on the pan and turn the heat down to low-ish. Set a timer for 15 minutes. Do not open the lid to peek at the rice during this time.

In the meantime, prepare your yoghurt sauce by simply stirring all the ingredients together.

Fill and boil the kettle again, then fill a small saucepan with freshly boiled water, add salt and cook the macaroni for 10 minutes or as per the packet instructions. When cooked, drain and leave to the side.

When the rice cooking time is up, remove from the heat and leave it to stand for another 5 minutes without removing the lid.

Take the lid off the rice pan, dot with the butter and give it a mix, then add the macaroni, onions and crispy spaghetti (keep a handful back for the topping). Give it all a good mix and taste for seasoning. Serve on a platter, with the tomato sauce spooned on top, blobs of the garlicky yoghurt, the remaining spaghetti strands and parsley.

Taco Night

Fish Finger Tacos

These Mexican-inspired fish finger open sandwiches are incredibly quick to make. Ideal for a casual dinner as part of a spread with the other taco filling recipes on pages 172–175 (or by themselves for a light dinner).

As it's nigh on impossible to buy small round soft corn tortillas in a cornershop (and too much of an undertaking for this book to make your own), we buy wheat tortilla wraps and cut them into 6–8 triangular pieces. (You could also use hard corn taco shells of the Old El Paso variety.)

Use battered or breaded fish, whatever you can find. There is absolutely no reason why you couldn't use a chicken nugget or two as well. Go wild with whatever riches the freezer section offers up to you.

Makes 12 tacos

Cooking time: 12 minutes
Preparation time: 15 minutes

For the quick-pickled red onion
1 small red onion
juice of ½ lime

For the salad
½ iceberg lettuce
good squeeze of mayonnaise
tiny squeeze of lime juice

For the quick tomato salsa
20 baby plum or cherry tomatoes
½ long red chilli
tiny splash of olive oil
pinch of salt
squeeze of lime juice

For the fish fingers and tacos
12 fish fingers
2 wheat tortilla wraps

For the quick guac
1 ripe avocado
juice of ½ lime
pinch of salt, or to taste

To serve
chilli sauce, such as sriracha
lots of lime quarters

For the pickled red onion, very thinly slice the red onion into rings (a mandoline will make quick work of this, but do watch your fingers), then place in a small bowl with the lime juice and mix. Set aside.

Preheat your grill to high (or as per fish finger packet instructions). While it is heating, put your mandoline or knife to work again and very finely shred the lettuce for the salad. We're talking McDonald's Big Mac-style shreds. Mix together with the mayonnaise and lime juice in a bowl, then set to one side.

For the salsa, dice the tomatoes and finely chop the chilli (discarding most of the seeds). Place in a bowl, along with a tiny splash of oil, a pinch of salt and a squeeze of lime juice – make sure to keep all that good tomato juice. Set aside.

Grill the fish fingers for 10–12 minutes until cooked, turning them halfway through.

Meanwhile, make the quick guac. Cut into the whole avocado in its skin, first lengthways, then a couple of times widthways, then discard the stone and push the flesh hedgehog fashion out into a small bowl. Discard the skin. Squeeze over the lime juice and add the salt to taste. Mix together without totally mushing the avo.

Preheat the oven to 180°C/gas 4.

Remove the fish fingers from the grill and cut them in half at a jaunty angle.

Now to the tacos. If they are big, then cut the tortillas in half with a knife or scissors, then cut each half into 3 equal-ish triangular pieces. If they are smaller, cut them in half, and then in half again (in triangles). Warm in the oven very briefly – be careful as they will crisp quickly and you want them to remain pliable.

Remove the tortilla pieces from the oven and place on a large platter, then top each one with some salad, then guac, then tomato salsa, and finally 2 fish finger halves. Top with pickled red onion rings.

Serve with chilli sauce and lime quarters, beer and napkins to protect against the inevitable shirt spillages.

The Whole Tamale

*If you want to mix your taco toppings up a bit you can make it a feast
by serving bowls of fried beans, roasted sweetcorn and tomato salad,
roasted carrot and beetroot salad and pineapple salsa, alongside extra
bowls of the all-important tomato salsa, quick guacamole, pickled red
onions (see Fish Finger Tacos on page 170), sour cream or crème fraîche,
chilli sauce and chopped coriander.*

*You don't have to make all the recipes below, of course – pick and
choose the ones that appeal to you. Pair the black beans with pineapple
salsa, the roasted sweetcorn salad with quick guacamole, and the carrot
and beetroot salad with pickled red onions – or make up your own
combinations.*

*These are just a few ideas: you can always further bump up the spread
(and mix things up) by serving shredded cooked chicken breast, sliced
rare steak or grilled prawns as luxe toppings.*

Each of the following is enough to top 12 triangular tacos,
or serving approximately 4 people

Fried Beans

Preparation time: 5 minutes
Cooking time: 15 minutes

2 small onions
2 garlic cloves
1 tbsp olive oil

1 tsp ground cumin
1 tsp ground cinnamon
2 x 400g tins black beans in water (or red
    kidney beans if you can't find black beans)
salt, to taste

Fincly chop the onions and garlic, then add to a large pan in which you've heated the oil. Fry for
around 5 minutes on a medium to high heat. If they go a bit brown and crispy, that's fine, but
don't let them burn. Add the cumin and cinnamon and fry for a further minute.

Drain and rinse the beans, but save a small amount (around ½ tinful) of their liquid in one of
the tins. Pour the beans and reserved liquid into the pan and cook on a high heat until the liquid
starts to reduce down and the beans turn mushy, stirring occasionally. Season with salt to taste.

Pineapple Salsa

Preparation time: 5 minutes

1 jalapeño or green chilli
1 tin (around 235g, depending on brand) sliced pineapple
5cm piece of cucumber
juice of ½ lime
large handful of mint leaves, finely chopped
large handful of coriander leaves, chopped
large pinch of salt

Seed and finely chop the jalapeño. Drain and chop the pineapple into small chunks (squeeze out as much excess juice as you can). Cut the cucumber into 4 pieces lengthways, cut out most of the seeds, then cut each long piece in half again, and chop into chunks similar in size to the pineapple. Mix the pineapple, jalapeño and cucumber together in a bowl, along with the lime juice, chopped herbs and salt.

Roasted Sweetcorn and Tomato Salad

Preparation time: 5 minutes
Cooking time: 20 minutes

2 x 340g tins sweetcorn (get the salt-free type if you can)
2 tbsp olive oil
20 cherry tomatoes, halved
1 red chilli
30g pecorino or Parmesan
juice of 1 lime
large handful of mint leaves, finely chopped (optional)
salt, to taste

Preheat the oven to 230°C/gas 8.

Drain the sweetcorn, getting rid of as much excess moisture as possible. Decant it into an ovenproof dish and add the oil and tomatoes. Give everything a good shake to mix it up and roast for 20 minutes, then take out and leave to cool.

Meanwhile, seed and finely dice the chilli and coarsely grate the cheese. Once the sweetcorn mix is cool, stir in the chilli, cheese and lime juice, then add salt to taste, before adding the mint, if using.

Roasted Carrot and Beetroot Salad

Preparation time: 5 minutes
Cooking time: 30 minutes

1½ tbsp groundnut oil
3 large carrots
4 ready-cooked beetroot

2 tbsp honey
¼ tsp dried chilli flakes
good crumbling of feta cheese (about 50g)
large handful of coriander,
    chopped (optional)

Preheat the oven to 230°C/gas 8. Add the oil to an ovenproof dish and put in the oven to heat.

Peel the carrots, then cut into slanted slices around 1cm thick. Halve these slices lengthways, and quarter any larger pieces. Cut the beets to a similar size.

Put the carrots and beets into the heated ovenproof dish, drizzle over the honey and sprinkle with the chilli flakes, then roast for 30 minutes.

Remove from the oven and leave to cool before crumbling in the feta, then mixing together with the coriander, if using.

Aubergine Lasagne

Not. Diet. Food.

Serves 4 — 6

Preparation time: 15 minutes
Cooking time: 1 hour 10 minutes

2 aubergines
3 tbsp extra-virgin olive oil, plus extra for
  cooking and drizzling
800g good-quality sausages (usually
  2 packets)

1 tsp dried thyme
1 bay leaf
3 x 400g tins chopped tomatoes
200ml red wine
150g dried lasagne sheets
sprinkling of grated Parmesan
salt and freshly ground black pepper

Preheat the oven to 180°C/gas 4.

Slice half an aubergine lengthways into thin slices, about 5mm thick. Chop the remaining whole and half aubergine into little dice and set aside. Brush both sides of the aubergine slices with the oil and place in an ovenproof dish. Sprinkle with salt and then bake for 15 minutes until soft.

While the aubergine slices are cooking, put a large pan on a medium heat, and add a little drizzle of olive oil. Squeeze out all of the sausagemeat from their skins and add to the pan. Use a wooden spoon to break up the sausagemeat into a mince (this gets easier as it cooks). After about 15 minutes, add the thyme, followed by the bay leaf, tomatoes, wine, remaining diced aubergines and a sprinkling of salt and pepper. Lower the heat and leave to simmer, uncovered, for 10 minutes, stirring occasionally.

Oil an ovenproof lasagne dish. Set 3 roughly evenly-sized cooked aubergine slices aside for the topping, then begin to layer your lasagne. Start with an even layer of sausage sauce, spooning it over the base of the dish, followed by some lasagne sheets and some of the remaining aubergine slices, and so forth. Finish with a layer of sausage sauce, topped by the 3 reserved aubergine slices. Drizzle over some oil and a sprinkling of Parmesan.

Bake for 40 minutes until golden, then serve. A mustardy lettuce and tomato salad on the side would be nice.

COMFORTING DINNERS WITH LEFTOVER POTENTIAL

Sometimes, for whatever reason, it feels darn good to take the time to put something delicious together for dinner. These are the days and nights when rather than rushing to get something on to the table, you find yourself calmed by methodical chopping and prepping, your mind focused on the immediate task. And, once things are baking or simmering away, you can be comforted by the knowledge that something really good is on its way and that, even though there is a little wait, that's all you now have to do.

Bakes, stews and soups aren't just the preserve of the weekend. And you don't need a leg of lamb or a shoulder of pork slow-cooking in the oven to send mouth-watering, comforting aromas through your house. This chapter celebrates the cornershop and convenience store bakes, broths and stews that give us that restful glow and nourished feeling that things cooked in a big pot usually bring. While the quantities aren't all enormous, all of these recipes taste good the next day, making them ideal packed lunch fodder.

Squash Minestrone with Kale Salsa Verde

This satisfying soup is perfect for evenings when there's more than a nip in the air. If you can't find squash, swap for courgettes instead.

Kale is fairly ubiquitous now, though you could also use cavolo nero or spring greens. If your local shop is the kind of place where the freshest green thing available is Apple Tango, use some jarred pesto instead — you'll save on prep time and washing up. If you want it to have a bit more of a 'zing', then add a splash of red wine vinegar.

Serves 4 — 6

Preparation time: 30 minutes
Cooking time: I hour (largely inactive)

For the soup
1 small butternut squash or ½ pumpkin
2 carrots
1 red onion
1 stick celery
3 garlic cloves
125g green beans (or use tinned)
bunch of kale (half is used for soup and the rest for salsa verde)
4 tbsp olive oil
sprig of rosemary or ½ tsp dried rosemary
200g tinned cherry tomatoes or tinned tomatoes or passata

1.75 litres hot vegetable stock or water
100g small pasta, like macaroni or ditali (or even broken up pieces of spaghetti)
1 x 400g tin cannellini beans
salt and freshly ground black pepper

For the salsa verde
½ bunch of kale (or use dark winter greens)
chunk of hard strong cheese, like Parmesan, grated
½ garlic clove, crushed
4 tbsp olive oil
pinch of salt
1 tsp capers
good splash of red wine vinegar

For the soup, peel and seed the squash, then chop into cubes of around 1.5cm. You want the pieces to be roughly the same size so they cook at the same speed. Finely(ish) chop the carrots, onion, celery and garlic, then top and tail the green beans and cut each bean into 2 or 3 shorter lengths (if especially long) so that you have small, bite-sized pieces. Wash the kale and chop roughly, discarding any very woody stalky bits. Divide into two piles and set aside.

Add the oil to a casserole pot and cook all the prepped vegetables (except the green beans and kale) for 15 minutes on a medium to low heat (i.e. not hot enough for them to brown too quickly or catch), with a pinch of salt and the rosemary. Add the tomatoes and cook for a couple of minutes. Add the hot stock or water and simmer gently, uncovered, for around 25 minutes.

To make the salsa verde, using a hand-held blender or food processor, whizz up half of the kale with the cheese (add this to taste), garlic, oil, pinch of salt and, lastly, the capers and red wine vinegar. Stop when it's still a bit chunky, taste and add more of anything, if necessary.

When the vegetables in the soup are tender, heat some water, with a pinch of salt, in a small pan until boiling, then add your small pasta of choice and cook for half the time given on the packet. (At this point you could give the soup the briefest of blends, to thicken it, if you wanted.)

While the pasta is cooking, drain and rinse the cannellini beans, and add to the soup, along with the green beans and the remaining chopped kale. When the pasta is done, drain, and add that too. Check the seasoning, – add some pepper – add a splash more water, if necessary, and leave to simmer gently for 5 minutes.

Serve the soup with the salsa verde in a separate bowl on the side, so everyone can help themselves.

Chickpea Dal with Butter Rice

Delicious, comforting, yet subtly complex, this is more warming and spiced than spicy.

Serves 3 — 4

Preparation time: 20 minutes
Cooking time: 35 minutes

For the dal
1 onion
1 heaped tsp cumin seeds
3–4 tbsp olive oil
1 garlic clove
thumb-sized piece of ginger, peeled
  and grated
3 x 400g tins chickpeas
1 tsp ground turmeric
1 tsp ground coriander
350ml chicken or vegetable stock
juice of 1 lime

For the rice
225g basmati rice
40g butter
1 onion
1 cinnamon stick
350ml hot chicken or vegetable stock
salt and freshly ground black pepper

natural yoghurt and corriander leaves,
  to serve

Start with the rice: place in a sieve and run under the cold tap. Rub the grains between your fingers to get rid of some of the starch, then leave to soak in a bowl of lightly salted warm water while you get on with the dal.

For the dal, finely chop the onion, and place a heavy-bottomed saucepan on a medium heat. Dry-fry the cumin seeds in the pan for a minute or two. Add the oil, followed by the onion, and cook for about 8–10 minutes, stirring frequently, until the onion has softened and is brown at the edges. Thinly slice the garlic and add to the pan, along with the ginger. Turn the heat down.

Briefly back to the rice: in a separate, high-rimmed frying pan, gently melt the butter. Thinly slice the onion and add to the pan, along with the cinnamon stick, snapped in half, and leave to slowly cook until golden and crispy. This takes around 15–20 minutes.

Now, back to the dal. Put the kettle on to boil (for your stock) and check the cooking onions and garlic aren't looking too dry in the saucepan (adding some extra oil if need be). Drain and

rinse the chickpeas and blend in a large bowl until you have a smooth purée, then stir into the saucepan. Add the turmeric and coriander and keep stirring. Make up the stock with the boiling water from the kettle, then gradually add to the saucepan. Leave the dal to simmer, uncovered, for 5–10 minutes, then remove from the heat and leave it to sit until your rice is ready.

Back to the rice again: drain the soaking grains and add to the buttery cooked onions, heat turned up. Fry for a minute before covering with the hot stock, followed by a lid or some foil. Turn the heat down, then cook for 15 minutes, until tender and all the liquid has been absorbed.

When you are about to serve, squeeze the lime juice into the dal, then taste to check the seasoning, adjusting if necessary. Serve with the butter rice and some yoghurt and corriander on top.

Baked Sweet Potatoes with Chorizo, Two Ways

Spicy Chorizo Chickpeas

This – and the following recipe – both call for minimal prep, a fair amount of cooking time, but a maximum return on your investment. We all know that a baked potato is worth the wait. We also know that the best baked potatoes are made at home.

Enjoy any leftover chorizo chickpeas with bread or toast. (Cool any leftovers before storing in the fridge for up to a day. Reheat gently until piping hot before serving.)

Serves 2

Preparation time: 15 minutes
Cooking time: 1 hour

2 sweet potatoes
2 tbsp olive oil, plus extra for the potatoes
1 tsp sea salt
2 small red onions
2 garlic cloves
1 red pepper, seeded
15cm chunk of chorizo

½ tsp dried chilli flakes
¾ tsp ground cumin
1 heaped tbsp tomato purée
1 x 400g tin plum tomatoes or 1 x 400g carton passata
2 x 400g tins chickpeas
2 heaped tsp Colman's or English mustard
splash of Worcestershire sauce
salt and freshly ground black pepper

Preheat the oven to 240°C/gas 9.

Rub the sweet potatoes all over with some oil and the sea salt. Place on a baking tray and bake for 50 minutes–1 hour (keep an eye on them as the cooking time will depend on the size of the potatoes).

Meanwhile, finely chop the red onions, garlic and red pepper. Remove the skin from the chorizo and slice lengthways into 4, then slice widthways into small-ish pieces. You could also just rip the meat off in rough hunks. Set aside.

Add the measured oil to a large, deep pan and fry the onions, garlic and red pepper on a medium heat until they soften, around 7 minutes. Make sure they don't stick to the pan. At this point, add the spices, cook for a couple of minutes, then add the chorizo. Cook until the fat starts to run, then add the tomato purée and cook for a couple more minutes. Add the tomatoes, breaking them up with your hand as you pour them into the pan. Fill the tomato tin with water and add to the pan – do this twice.

Drain and rinse the chickpeas and add to the pan, along with salt and pepper. Bring to the boil and cook, uncovered, on a medium to high heat for 10 minutes, then add the mustard, Worcestershire sauce and more water if it's reduced down a lot and needs more liquid. Cook for a further 20 minutes, then taste and adjust the seasoning as you think necessary. You shouldn't be able to really taste the mustard   it will just add a mysterious sort of creaminess.

By this point your potatoes should be ready. Cut them open, mash up the flesh, and season, before adding a good couple of ladlefuls of the chickpeas.

Stuffed with Chorizo and Sour Cream with Quick Slaw

If you can't find sweet potatoes, of course, normal baking potatoes will do: you may need to cook them for 10–15 minutes longer. Similarly, substitute chorizo for smoked bacon, cut into chunks, if your local is out of stock.

Serves 2

Preparation time: 10 minutes
Cooking time: 1 hour 20 minutes

For the stuffed potatoes
2 sweet potatoes
olive oil, for the potatoes and drizzling
1 tsp sea salt
100g chorizo sausage
4 tbsp sour cream, plus extra for serving

squeeze of lemon juice
2 tbsp crumbled feta cheese
freshly ground black pepper, to taste

For the quick slaw
1 red onion
¼ white cabbage
small drizzle of extra-virgin olive oil
juice of ½ lemon

Preheat the oven to 240°C/gas 9.

Rub the sweet potatoes all over with some oil and sea salt. Place on a baking tray and bake for 50 minutes–1 hour (keep an eye on them as the cooking time will depend on the size of the potatoes).

Meanwhile, chop the chorizo into little chunks. Place a frying pan on a medium heat (no need for oil as the chorizo sausage contains enough to cook with already) and fry for about 7 minutes until crispy in bits. Remove and set aside.

After the potatoes have been cooking for about an hour, remove from the oven and cut in half. Scoop out the potato flesh and place in a bowl, leaving the skins intact on the baking tray. Add the sour cream, another drizzle of oil and a squeeze of lemon juice to the potato flesh, along with some black pepper. Mash and mix well, then stir in the chorizo, reserving a tablespoon for the topping.

Spoon the filling back into the 4 potato halves, and top with the remaining chunks of chorizo and the crumbled feta. Finish with a final drizzle of oil and a sprinkling of black pepper. Bake for a further 20 minutes.

While the stuffed potatoes are cooking, prepare the slaw. Cut the onion in half, then slice as thinly as you can, along with the white cabbage. Place in a serving bowl and drizzle over the oil and lemon juice. Finally, sprinkle over some salt and mix well.

When the potato toppings have gone golden and crispy, they are ready to serve alongside the crunchy slaw and extra sour cream.

Cider-Baked Sausages and Apples

Our friend Chloe cooked this classic dish for us during a midweek dinner party in Kennington once. We were so impressed with the results and simplicity of the recipe that we have recreated this countless times since. Although there's always a space for a Richmond Sausage in our fry-ups, this recipe definitely calls for posher supermarket own-brand pork sausages.

Serves 4

Preparation time: 5 minutes
Cooking time: 40 minutes

12 pork sausages
4 eating apples, such as Braeburn or Cox's, left whole (uncored)
2 red onions, quartered

1 onion, quartered
4 garlic cloves, unpeeled
4 bay leaves
1 or 2 sprigs of rosemary
1 tsp dried thyme
drizzle of olive oil
about 400ml apple cider (not fizzy)

Preheat the oven to 180°C/gas 4.

Place all of the ingredients, minus the oil and cider, in an ovenproof dish or roasting tin. Now drizzle over some oil, mixing well. Bake for 20 minutes.

Remove the tray from the oven and pour over enough cider to partly cover everything, then return to the oven and bake for another 20 minutes, or until the sausages are cooked and the apples are nicely exploded and caramelised.

Serve with mashed potato or crusty bread.

Thyme, Chorizo and Leek Broth

This warming broth errs on the side of stew. If you're fastidious about presentation, ensure your potatoes, leeks and chorizo are sliced evenly, otherwise the rustic look is just as pleasing. Serve with generously buttered baguette or the Grilled Cheese Sandwich (see page 200), along with a large glass of ale. Can't find chorizo? Use snipped bits of smoked bacon, or lardons instead. Can't find leeks? Use a combination of carrot, celery and onion instead for a nice variation.

Serves 4

Preparation time: 10 minutes
Cooking time: 25 minutes

2 leeks
100g chorizo sausage
knob of butter (optional)
200g potatoes

1 x 400g tin butter beans, drained and rinsed
1 bay leaf
1 tsp paprika
½ tsp dried thyme
750ml boiling water
salt and freshly ground black pepper

Cut a slit lengthways down each leek and fan out under the tap to rinse out any grit. Thinly slice into circular segments about 5mm wide.

Place a heavy-bottomed casserole pot on a medium heat. Slice the chorizo into thin segments and add to the now hot pan (the chorizo won't need oil). When the fat from the chorizo begins to run, stir in your sliced leeks and a generous pinch of salt and pepper. Leave the leeks to soften for 4–5 minutes. If you're worried they might catch, melt in the knob of butter and put the lid on the casserole.

Meanwhile, put the kettle on to boil and wash the potatoes, peeling if you wish, then slice into 1cm cubes. Add the potatoes to the pan, along with the drained butter beans, the bay leaf, paprika and thyme and mix for a minute or two.

Add the measured boiling water to the pan and leave the broth to simmer, lid off, for 10 minutes, or until your little potato cubes are cooked. Leave for a few minutes and then taste to check the seasoning, adding a little extra salt, if necessary. Remove the bay leaf and serve with crusty bread.

Aubergine, Butter Bean and Feta Bake

This recipe has two stages so takes a little longer to cook, but the results are definitely worth the wait. Don't have aubergines? Most other roastable veg will do: red onions, courgettes, parsnips – even mushrooms. Just adjust the initial roasting time as necessary.

Serves 4

Preparation time: 10 minutes
Cooking time: 50 minutes

2 large aubergines
200g cherry tomatoes
3 tbsp olive oil

100g couscous
1 x 400g tin butter beans, drained and rinsed
1 tsp dried thyme
4 tbsp crumbled feta cheese
3 tbsp fresh or dried breadcrumbs (optional)
salt and freshly ground black pepper

Preheat the oven to 180°C/gas 4.

Cut the aubergines into 2cm chunks and add to a roasting tin, along with the cherry tomatoes. Drizzle over 2 tablespoons of the oil, sprinkle over some salt and pepper, and then bake for 35 minutes, or until the aubergine is golden and slightly caramelised in places and the cherry tomatoes have burst.

Meanwhile, boil a kettleful of water for your couscous. Measure the couscous into an ovenproof pie dish and pour over enough boiling water to cover (aim for 1 – 2mm above the top of the couscous). Cover with a tea towel for a few minutes, then once fluffy and cooked, fork the couscous and add the remaining oil and some salt. Stir in the drained butter beans and the thyme, then crumble over most of the feta (saving the rest to sprinkle on top).

Once the roasted vegetables are ready, stir straight into the couscous mixture. Top with the breadcrumbs, if using, and crumble over the remaining feta. Bake for a further 15 minutes until the feta is melted and golden brown in places. Serve with a green salad.

Roasted Mediterranean Vegetables with Rice, Pesto and Feta

This dish is probably the ultimate cornershop recipe in that all the ingredients, bar the tomatoes, are swappable. Exchange the feta for goat's cheese, the rice for barley, and so on. Most vegetables taste delicious in this, so you can use any combination of what you have available. We've suggested our favoured mix. But do stick to using the tomatoes as you need something saucy and juicy to bring all the ingredients together.

Serves 4 — 6

Preparation time: 10 minutes
Cooking time: 40 minutes

1.2kg roastable vegetables (approximately
 2 red onions, 4 tomatoes, 2 courgettes,
 1–2 aubergines)
4 garlic cloves, unpeeled

about 6 tbsp olive oil
pinch of dried thyme or oregano
320g long-grain rice
1 x 190g jar red pesto
50g feta cheese
1–2 tbsp pine nuts
salt and freshly ground black pepper

Preheat the oven to 190°C/gas 5.

Quarter the red onions, and chop all of the remaining vegetables into 2cm chunks. Arrange on 2 baking trays and then pop 2 garlic cloves in their skins on each. Drizzle over a generous amount of oil, then sprinkle over the thyme and some salt and pepper. Use your hands to give the vegetables a good mix, then pop in the oven for 40 minutes, giving them a turn with a metal spatula from time to time.

After you've put the veg in the oven, attend to your rice: place the rice in a pan of salted water and bring to the boil, then lower the heat to a simmer. Cook for 20–25 minutes, testing the grains of rice a few times towards the end.

When the rice is cooked, drain, then put it in a large serving dish. Stir in the red pesto, then leave to the side, keeping it warm.

When your vegetables are nicely golden or caramelised and charred in bits, they are ready. Remove from the oven and spread over the top of the rice, squeezing the garlic flesh out of the skins. Top with the crumbled feta cheese and a sprinkling of pine nuts.

COMFORTING DINNERS WITH LEFTOVER POTENTIAL

Tomato Soup with Grilled Cheese Sandwich

Yes, you could just buy a tin of Heinz, but there is something pleasing about the ritual of making soup from scratch. Plus, the longer cooking time means that the simmering pot will warm up your kitchen, filling it with good, comforting smells. Serve with the Grilled Cheese Sandwich (see page 200).

Serves 2

Preparation time: 5 minutes
Cooking time: 25–30 minutes

45g butter
2 small onions, cut in half

3 garlic cloves, peeled
sprig of thyme or ½ tsp dried thyme
2 x 400g tins plum tomatoes
salt and freshly ground black pepper

Add the butter to a saucepan and melt on a low heat, then add the onions and garlic. Leave to cook for a couple of minutes, then add the thyme and tomatoes, squishing the tomatoes through your hand to break them down as you add them. Fill both tins with water and add to the pan. Cook, uncovered, on a medium heat for 25 – 30 minutes, until the onions start to disintegrate. (You may need to turn the heat down a bit towards the end.)

Remove from the heat and cool slightly, then blend with a hand-held stick blender. Season to taste. Add more water if the consistency seems too thick, and reheat if necessary. Serve with lots of black pepper and extra salt, if necessary, and a Grilled Cheese Sandwich (see page 200) alongside.

BREAD AHEAD

It can be difficult to buy really good bread in the evenings — often pitta or a ready-to-bake baguette is as good as it gets. While that works for many sandwiches, it's not ideal here. We often buy a loaf of sourdough or rye when out wandering at the weekend, and then keep a few slices in a sealed bag in the freezer, ready for any weeknight grilled cheese cravings. When you want to use it, just defrost the slices in the toaster or oven for a minute or two.

Grilled Cheese Sandwich

Nothing beats tomato soup with butter and Marmite-laden toast on the side for dipping – except perhaps an oozy grilled cheese sandwich. In fact, good though it is, the soup is often little more than an excuse to make this sandwich to eat 'on the side'.

We wouldn't serve sliced American cheese on a cheeseboard, granted, but it melts pleasingly here.

Makes 2 sandwiches

Preparation time: 5 minutes
Cooking time: 10 minutes

40g Cheddar of your choice
8 slices of Kraft singles, or other American sliced processed cheese (optional)

4 slices of bread (a sturdy sort, such as sourdough, is ideal)
2 tbsp mayonnaise
knob of butter

Grate the Cheddar. Lay 2 slices of American cheese on one slice of bread, top with half of the grated Cheddar, then top the other slice of bread with 2 more slices of American cheese. Tuck in any unwieldy overhanging cheese. Sandwich the 2 slices of bread together (so you should have bread, American cheese, Cheddar, American cheese, bread). Spread a thin layer of mayo on each outer surface of bread. Repeat to make the second sandwich.

Melt the butter in a heavy-bottomed frying pan large enough to accommodate both sandwiches. When sizzling (but not madly smoking), add the sandwiches. Press down on them with a large metal spatula and cook for around 3 – 4 minutes, before flipping over and cooking for another 3–4 minutes on the other side. Eat while still hot, but not so molten that you burn the roof of your mouth.

SOMETHING SWEET

No one truly needs to make a pudding for a speedy weeknight dinner. A sneaky square or two of Fruit & Nut is enough to satisfy most sugary cravings. Having people round? You know what to do (bring out the big guns in the individually packaged form of After Eights, obviously).

But though they might be few and far between, there are times when you might feel like creating your own little sweet something. Perhaps you've just watched *The Great British Bake Off*. Or maybe you're having a few friends over and thought you'd pick up a pudding on the way home, but found that nothing on offer took your fancy, and – horror of horrors – the shop was out of the Häagen-Dazs you'd set your heart on. You need to pull something together with the minimum of whisking and sifting. Our Frostie Florentines (see page 204),

made with largely store cupboard ingredients, could be the answer – grab some white chocolate (a few Milkybars will do the trick) and salted peanuts on the way home, and you're probably good to go.

Other times, you might find that the emergency chocolate stash has been mysteriously emptied. This is when you need to attack the dark depths of the cupboard or freezer, to find that ferreted away jar of Nutella that can be transformed into a warming hot chocolatey shot in moments, or the end of a forgotten tub of vanilla ice cream, made into a luxe dessert with a sprinkling of chopped pistachios or a quick home-made caramel sauce.

If all else fails, the cornershop is a veritable treasure chest of instant desserts: custard, fruit cocktails, sticky toffee pudding in a tin… just crack out your tin opener.

Florentines, Two Ways

It took us years to work out that florentines don't have to be relegated – along with Terry's Chocolate Oranges and Matchmakers – to the annual realms of Christmas treats. You can knock them up yourself with relative ease: the only annoying thing is having to poke them back into shape.

Here are two recipes, one for a traditional fruit 'n' nut florentine (see recipe overleaf), and one for a slightly trashier version, using white chocolate and everyone's favourite cereal from the variety pack, Frosties. You can guess which type disappears first.

The types of nuts, dried fruits and, indeed, breakfast cereal, are of course completely interchangeable.

Both recipes make around 12 — 14 florentines

Frostie Florentines

An honest breakdown:

Preparation time: 10 minutes (for measuring)

Cooking time: 25 minutes (including butter and chocolate melting)

Florentine sculpting time: 10 minutes

Cooling time: 45 minutes (including initial pre-chocolate cooling period)

For the dry ingredients
50g frosties, broken up (or crunchy nut cornflakes or indeed regular cornflakes)
80g salted peanuts
1 tbsp plain flour

For the 'wet' ingredients
50g butter
50ml golden syrup
50g caster sugar
good pinch of salt

To finish
100g white chocolate, broken into chunks

More Traditional and Elegant Florentines

Preparation and cooking times on
page 204

For the dry ingredients
50g flaked almonds
40g pistachios, roughly chopped
40g dried fruit (dried cherries, prunes, figs or
  sultanas), chopped
1 tbsp ground almonds or plain flour

For the 'wet' ingredients
50g butter
50ml honey
50g caster sugar
good pinch of salt

To finish
100g milk chocolate (or dark if you want to
  be really sophisticated), broken
  into chunks

METHOD FOR BOTH

Preheat the oven to 160°C/gas 3 and line 2 baking trays with greaseproof paper, ready for action.

Mix the dry ingredients together in a bowl.

Add the 'wet' ingredients to a medium-sized saucepan and place on a low heat. Cook, stirring, if necessary, for around 5 minutes, until everything is melted and incorporated and the mixture has a thick, almost custard-like appearance. It may be bubbling when it reaches this point – that's fine. Remove from the heat and quickly mix in the dry ingredients.

Work with the mix right away as it will get harder to use as it cools (it's a good idea to warm it again when you get to the second batch). Add a heaped teaspoonful of the mixture to a lined baking tray in a blob – spread the blob out as each one will expand in the oven a lot. You should do no more than 4 per sheet (unless you have a weirdly huge baking tray) although you can bake two batches at once. Make sure each blob has an equal-ish amount of nuts and enough syrupy mix to bind it together.

Set a timer and bake for 12 minutes, keeping an eagle eye on them. They will start to spread out quickly – if they are going too wild and spreading into each other, take them out and, using a knife, gently poke them back into an appropriate circular florentine shape (this is easier if you leave them to cool for a moment) before popping back in the oven.

When the 12 minutes are up, remove from the oven, then poke the florentines back into shape (again, leave them to cool for a minute or so first). Clean your poking knife, or use a new one, to make it easier. Once the florentines are firm enough to keep their shape, transfer to a wire rack and leave to cool completely. Repeat until all the mixture is used up.

Whatever type of chocolate you're using to finish, melt it in a heatproof bowl set over a pan of barely simmering water (making sure the water doesn't touch the base of the bowl) on a low heat, keeping an eye on it.

Brush the flat undersides of the cooled and hardened florentines with the melted chocolate, then leave to chill in the fridge for about 30 minutes before serving. Store any leftovers (if there are any!) in an airtight container.

VANILLA CASTER SUGAR

If you ever use vanilla pods in your more ambitious weekend baking, retain the husks and keep in a clean jar with your caster sugar. The oils will infuse the sugar and you will have vanilla-infused caster sugar at hand for all manner of things, including florentines.

Cornershop Lime Pie

You may not have cause to buy it often, but surely one of the most glorious ingredients to grace any shop's shelves is condensed milk. Boil it in the can, on its side, in a large pot of water to make dulce de leche (if you happen to have a spare 3 hours), or just pour it into a bowl and mix with lime and cream to make this stripped-back version of Key Lime Pie.

Serves 6 — 8

Preparation time: 10 minutes, plus
    1 hour chilling
Cooking time: 5 minutes (to melt butter)

For the base
50g butter
100g Ritz crackers (you could use
    digestives instead)

For the filling
1 x 227ml carton double cream
1 x 397g tin condensed milk
finely grated zest and juice of 4 large limes

First make your base. Melt the butter in a small saucepan. Add the crackers, crushing them with your hand as you pour them into the pan – don't obliterate them though as it's nice to have a few chunky bits. Mix together, then line the bottom of 6 – 8 small tumbler glasses with an equal amount of the mixture, around 1 heaped teaspoon (6 is a good portion, but you could easily stretch the mix out to make 8 smaller glasses). Press down on the mix with the back of a teaspoon, and leave the glasses to chill in the fridge.

For the filling, whip the cream in a bowl until it forms very soft peaks. Pour the condensed milk into a separate large bowl (scraping it all out), then add the zest of 3 limes and all the lime juice. Give it a good mix – it will look worryingly like scrambled eggs at first, then it will start to magically thicken and be okay. Fold in the whipped cream until well combined.

Spoon an equal amount of the filling mix into your glasses, and top with the remaining lime zest. Chill in the fridge for at least an hour before serving.

Rocky Road

If you want to make a gluten-free version of this, up the nut quantity and omit the biscuits.

Serves 6 — 8

Preparation time: 15 minutes, plus cooling and 2 hours setting
Cooking time: 6–8 minutes

120g butter, diced, plus extra for greasing

300g dark chocolate, broken into chunks
100g marshmallows
150g digestive biscuits
150g nuts (pistachios, walnuts, pecans, peanuts, etc)

Line a shallow 25cm square cake tin or pie dish with greaseproof paper, using a few dots of butter to affix on the underside.

Place the butter and chocolate in a heatproof bowl set over a pan of simmering water and melt, stirring frequently with a wooden spoon. Meanwhile, if the marshmallows are large, cut into smaller chunks. Place the biscuits in a freezer bag and bash with a rolling pin until you have small chunks and lots of crumbs.

Remove the bowl of now melted butter and chocolate from the pan and leave to cool slightly (about 5 minutes). Then, stir in your biscuits, nuts and marshmallows, mixing well to coat evenly.

Spread into your tin using the back of a wooden spoon to level out the top. Leave to cool completely, before popping in the fridge for a minimum of 2 hours. Once set, cut into squares using a sharp knife. It will keep for a few days in a sealed container.

Nutella Hot Chocolate

Of course you can buy instant hot chocolate in most shops. But sometimes it's only after dinner that you decide you want a sweet hit, and curse yourself for not having bought anything. This is when that forgotten jar of Nutella comes to the fore. You may think the suggested serving size a bit mean, but it's just enough to sate a sweet tooth, which is all this is about. Espresso cups lend a sort of elegance to something that is one step up from eating Nutella out of the jar with a spoon.

For each cup

'Cooking' (can it even be described as cooking?) time: 3½ minutes

allow ¾ of an espresso cupful of milk and
  2 tsp Nutella per person

tiny pinch of salt or dried chilli flakes, to taste
  (optional)

Gently heat the milk in a saucepan. When warm, stir in the Nutella – stir until it dissolves and looks like hot chocolate. Heat to your liking, but don't let it boil. Pour back into the espresso cup you used to measure the milk.

If you want, you can add a tiny pinch of salt, or a really teeny tiny pinch of dried chilli flakes to jazz it up.

Chai with Cardamom Shortbread

We are slightly obsessed with chai and would encourage you to experiment with the spice mix below to create your own signature tea. Make bigger batches of the spice mix (it will keep in a sealed jar for a few weeks) if you find yourself guzzling the stuff like Claret.

Serves 4 — 6

Preparation time: 10 minutes, plus cooling
Cooking time: 40 minutes

For the shortbread
1 green cardamom pod
150g plain flour
100g butter, at room temperature
50g caster sugar, plus extra for dusting

For the chai
2 green cardamom pods
2 cloves
1 tsp freshly ground black pepper
1 tsp ground ginger
¼ tsp ground cinnamon
grating of nutmeg
1 star anise
4 black tea bags or 4 tsp black tea leaves
600ml whole milk
150ml water
sugar, to serve (optional)

To make the shortbread:

Preheat the oven to 180°C/gas 4 and line a baking tray with parchment paper.

Remove the cardamom seeds from the pod and crush to a powder using a pestle and mortar. Sift the flour into a bowl and mix in the ground cardamom.

Cream the butter and sugar together in a separate large bowl, then add the flour and cardamom. Mix with a wooden spoon until combined, then roll lightly into a paste about 1cm thick.

Place the rolled paste on to your lined baking tray, and shape into a circle using an upside-down tart tin or your fingers. Use a knife to score some slices: this will make it easy to break into pieces later. Prick the mixture with a fork, then bake for 30–40 minutes until going golden.

When ready, transfer to a wire rack and leave to cool completely, before breaking into biscuits and storing in a sealed container until you are ready to serve (it will keep for a few days).

To make the chai:

Remove the cardamom seeds from the pods and crush, along with the cloves, using a pestle and mortar. Add to a pan with a spout, along with all the remaining ingredients (except the sugar), and place on a low heat. Slowly bring to the boil, stirring occasionally. Strain and serve immediately, sweetened with sugar to taste, if you like.

Crispy Peanut Butter and Chocolate Truffles

The type of peanut butter is important here – ideally you don't want it to be too gloopy, which natural peanut butters often are. US brand Skippy is our favourite, and available in most supermarkets now, though sadly not all local shops (stock it please!), so we tend to bulk buy when we can.

Makes around 12 small 'truffles'

Preparation time: 10 minutes,
  plus 30 minutes setting
Cooking time: 6–8 minutes

10g butter
80g milk chocolate, broken into chunks

150g smooth peanut butter
good pinch of salt
50g icing sugar
30g cocoa pops, crushed
additional icing sugar or cocoa powder,
  to dust

Line a baking tray with greaseproof paper and set aside

Melt the butter and chocolate in a heatproof bowl set over a pan of simmering water. Once melted, remove the bowl from the pan and add the peanut butter and salt, mixing together with a spoon, then add the icing sugar and cocoa pops – put some effort into it so that it's properly mixed.

Dust a clean work surface with additional icing sugar or cocoa powder. Scoop up a heaped teaspoonful of the mix and drop on to the surface. Using your hands, roll along the surface and shape into a little ball. Try not to overwork it as the mixture will be sticky. Repeat until all the mix is used up. Dust over more icing sugar or cocoa powder, if necessary.

Put the balls on to the lined baking tray. Put in the fridge and leave to set for 30 minutes, or while you eat dinner.

Marshmallow Puffed Rice and Oat Cakes with Golden Syrup

A tasty way of using up the box of cereal you've had above your fridge for far too long. Probably not the most sophisticated of desserts but a yummy sweet treat nonetheless.

Makes 1 trayful/Serves about 8

Preparation time: 10 minutes,
   plus 30 minutes setting
Cooking time: 10 minutes

40g butter, plus extra for greasing

250g marshmallows
1 tbsp golden syrup
1 tsp vanilla extract
150g rice crispies
40g porridge oats

Line a medium-sized square pie dish or baking tin (we used a 15 x 20cm one) with greaseproof paper. Use a few dots of butter on the underside to affix.

Melt the butter in a heatproof bowl set over a pan of simmering water on a low heat. Add the marshmallows and stir with a wooden spoon until completely melted. Add the golden syrup and vanilla extract, then turn the heat off and remove the bowl from the pan.

Stir in the rice crispies and oats and once evenly coated, spoon into your prepared dish or tin, spreading into an even layer. Smooth the top with the back of a spoon as quickly as you can as this mixture goes very sticky, very quickly. If you're not quick enough and you can't get the top to go flat, wait 10 minutes for the mixure to set a little, then you should be able to push it into position with more ease.

Leave to set at room temperature for 30 minutes, before cutting into squares and storing in a sealed container until you are ready to eat (it will keep for a few days).

Pistachio and Vanilla Cheesecake

What you have here is a simple recipe that can look as classy or as 1970s as you wish: vary the toppings according to your mood or what you have available to you. Drained tinned peaches or tropical fruit salad are delish toppings, and things like pomegranate seeds (before you give us that look you can get them in mini supermarkets in the 'meal deal' sections – pre-seeded for your convenience and everything) or unsalted, crushed pistachios look glam. It's a little cake and there isn't a snowy mountain of cheese topping in our recipe, but that is just how we like it.

Serves 6

Preparation time: 20 minutes,
   plus 2 hours setting
Cooking time: 5 minutes (to melt butter)

75g butter, plus extra for greasing
200g digestive biscuits

50g icing sugar
seeds from 1 vanilla pod or 1 tsp
   vanilla extract
300g cream cheese (like Philadelphia)
100ml double cream
35g (unshelled weight) unsalted pistachio nuts

Grease and line the base of a 20cm springform tin with greaseproof paper.

Melt the butter in a pan. Place the biscuits in a freezer bag and bash with a rolling pin until you have just crumbs left. Pour the crumbs into the melted butter and mix well before popping into the bottom of the prepared tin. Use a wooden spoon to press it down firmly and evenly, then chill in the fridge for at least an hour.

Beat the icing sugar and vanilla into the cream cheese in a bowl, and then add the cream, mixing gently but well. Spread the mixture over the chilled buttery biscuit base, ensuring there are no air bubbles, then pop in the fridge for at least another hour.

About 10 minutes before you are ready to serve, take the cake out of the fridge. Carefully remove the tin by sitting the cake on a tin of beans or similar then popping the sides open and sliding them down. Then, using a sharp knife to prise it from the base, slip the cake on to a serving plate. Finally, shell then chop the pistachio nuts and sprinkle over the top.

Banoffee Messes with a Salted Caramel Sauce

Cream can be hard to come by in a cornershop so this is definitely more of a convenience store recipe. This recipe is our contribution to the 67976 variants of this classic Sussex-born pie.

Try substituting the bananas with tinned or fresh pineapple, as this fruit is also a firm friend of caramel.

Serves 4

Preparation time: 10 minutes,
 plus 20 minutes chilling
Cooking time: 15–20 minutes

For the banoffee messes
40g butter
200g ginger crunch biscuits
250ml double cream
2 ripe bananas

For the salted caramel sauce
40g butter
25g soft light brown sugar
25g caster sugar
25g golden syrup
75ml double cream
pinch of sea salt

To make the messes, first melt the butter in a pan. Place the ginger biscuits in a freezer bag and bash with a rolling pin until you have just crumbs left. Pour the crumbs into the melted butter and mix well before dividing between 4 bowls. Don't pack the crumb mixture too tightly into the bowls – keep it relatively loose, then place in the fridge to chill for 20 minutes.

While the buttery biscuit bases are chilling, make your salted caramel sauce. Place the butter, sugars and golden syrup in a pan on a low heat and melt, stirring with a wooden spoon to encourage the sugar to dissolve. Let it bubble for a few minutes, then stir in the cream. Cook for a further minute or two until it is all incorporated, then turn the heat off and add the salt. Set aside.

When you are ready to eat, finish the messes. Pour the cream into a bowl and whip until the texture is light and the volume has increased. Peel and slice the bananas, then fold the equivalent of 1½ bananas into the cream. (The remaining slices are for the topping.)

Remove the bowls from the fridge and divide the banana cream between them. Top with the remaining banana slices, then pour over the salted caramel sauce.

Things with Ice Cream

Not everyone has a sweet tooth, however there are some people for whom a meal is not a meal unless it's rounded off with something naughty. If you're cooking for such guests midweek, and are short of time, the easiest thing to do is pimp some good-quality vanilla ice cream with accessories.

Affogato

Place a scoop of ice cream in as many glasses as you have guests, and cover each with a shot and a half of freshly brewed espresso strength coffee. Eat tout de suite.

Nutty

Maybe it's a phase we're going through, but at the moment we find pistachio nuts look beautiful on pretty much anything – it's the edible glitter of the moment. Buy a packet of the unsalted variety, shell then finely chop, before sprinkling on ice cream. Hazelnuts or pecans are also lovely.

Baked Apples

Preheat the oven to 180°C/gas 4, then pop as many washed, cored eating apples as you have guests, on a baking tray. Fill the core holes with a tablespoon or so of soft light brown sugar and some raisins, then top each with a little knob of butter and a sprinkling of ground cinnamon. Bake for 40 minutes or until tender, before serving alongside a scoop of the cold stuff.

Biscuity Caramel

Make the Salted Caramel Sauce on previous page, minus the salt, and pour over scoops of ice cream studded with any nice biscuits you have: shortbread, amaretti, ginger crunch, etc.

Cornershop Pavlova

Pavlova has many advantages: good-looking, gluten-free AND requires minimal ingredients. Make the meringue well before you need the pavlova to be served as it takes 45 minutes to cook, then is best left in the oven to dry out for a further few hours.

Nestled next to the mushy peas and Fray Bentos in your local cornershop, there should be a selection of tinned sliced pineapple, peaches and pears – maybe even some lychees, if you're lucky. These are your ready-made cornershop pavlova toppings.

As with the Pistachio and Vanilla Cheesecake (page 219), the cornershop is your oyster when it comes to toppings so feel free to use fresh fruit like blueberries and strawberries here instead.

Serves 4 — 6

Preparation time: 20 minutes, plus cooling
Cooking time: 45 minutes

For the meringue base
4 egg whites
200g caster sugar

For the topping
200ml double or whipping cream
1 vanilla pod or 1 tsp vanilla extract
1 x 400g tin fruit of your choice (or 400g mixed tinned fruit), in syrup or juice

First make your meringue base. Preheat the oven to 140°C/gas 1 and line a baking tray with a piece of parchment paper cut to size.

Place the egg whites in a clean mixing bowl, preferably glass, and begin to whisk. After a few minutes, begin to add the sugar a few tablespoons at a time, and continue whisking until you have a glossy mixture forming stiff peaks. This can take 10 minutes or longer.

Once ready, artfully spoon your meringue on to the prepared baking tray (use a blob of the mixture to affix the underside of the parchment to the baking tray). Dolloping the mixture will ensure you have pretty peaks. Bake for 45 minutes. When the time is up, turn the oven off but leave the meringue in the oven (with the door closed) to dry for a further few hours, if possible.

When you are ready to serve the pav, attend to the topping. Pour the cream into a bowl, add the vanilla seeds scraped from the pod (or the vanilla extract), then lightly whisk to increase the volume a little – until thick (but don't overwhip).

Place your meringue base on your serving dish, then spoon over the whipped cream. Drain your tinned fruit and artfully pour over the top. Enjoy immediately.

Frozen Banana Ice Cream

Cornershop cooking – especially of the sweet variety – doesn't always go hand in hand with clean living (Haribo Tangfastic, anyone?). But this incredibly easy two-ingredient 'ice cream' shows that it doesn't have to be bad to be good. If you wanted to complicate matters, you could add some smooth peanut butter.

Serves 2

Preparation time: 8 minutes, plus a few hours freezing

3 bananas
½ tsp ground cinnamon, plus more to finish

To freeze the bananas, peel and thinly slice them, transfer to a freezer bag, seal and freeze for a few hours – you could also put them into the freezer first thing in the morning so they're ready when you come home.

When you're ready to eat, blend the frozen bananas in a food processor or using a hand-held stick blender in a bowl, until smooth and creamy – just a few minutes. Add the cinnamon and blend again. Serve immediately, with a sprinkle of more cinnamon on top.

ACKNOWLEDGEMENTS

Rowan Yapp – we couldn't ask for a kinder or more impressively capable editor who just gets it, whatever weird thing 'it' may be on any given day.

The brilliant people at Square Peg and Vintage, who are such a pleasure to work with – Rosemary Davidson, Simon Rhodes, Lisa Gooding, Minty Nicholson.

Charlotte Bland – outstandingly talented photographer and wonderfully kind person. We're so happy you have been part of making this book.

Charlotte Heal and Kat Jenkins – for the perfect design.

Jon 'Ari' Elek – for many things. This was your idea first, thank you.

Tim Sandford – for being generally wonderful and generous. Especially with lifts, and guac egg hash modelling.

Our parents – for all their support and advice. We love you so much. Our siblings too.

Françoise Craig – for all her recipe testing and detailed notes. We can't thank you enough!

Paul Missing – for meticulous aubergine recipe testing. If it meets your exacting standards then we know it must be okay.

Tom Elek – for heroically testing some of the lengthier recipes and helping us weed out some howlers!

And Youki Crump, for graciously volunteering to test some of the 98% cheese recipes.

Our brilliant, hardworking kitchen helpers (and often unwitting models): Etta Howells, Nathalie Dubant, Tim Sandford, Josephine Maxwell, Jake Missing, and Scarlet Evans.

Not unwitting but brilliant models: Julia Jeuvell, Tom Bennett and Lareina Lin.

Tamsin English and Nick Sidwell, our dear friends – for letting us take over their beautiful house for some of the shoots.

Frank Carson – for sharing his perfect tuna melt recipe, and for taking Sophie on an inspirational sandwich tour of New York, along with Susannah 'Sandwich' Webb.

Mina Holland, our editor at the Guardian – for her support and friendship.

Juliet Annan – mentor in matters delicious and otherwise.

Chloe Shearing and Harriet Maxwell of Closet and Botts in Lewes. Thank you for lending us your beautiful things and letting us rummage behind the scenes of your wonderful shop. Also, The Lacquer Chest in Kensington – for having really great stuff.

The minicabs of London – or at least the ones who let us get in with 97 bags of shopping and half our kitchens without batting an eyelid.

Our favourite local shops and cornershops – for always coming up with the goods. 50% of our income is yours, forever.

Special thanks to the shops that allowed us to take photos: Newington Green Fruit and Veg, Costcutter Newington Green, Ege Supermarket, North London Wine Cellar, Grosvenor Wines in Canonbury.

ABOUT THE AUTHORS

Caroline Craig is a London based food writer. She co-wrote The Little Book of Lunch with Sophie Missing and is a columnist for Guardian Cook. She also recently contributed to Teas, Tonics and Tipples, published by Kew Gardens.

Sophie Missing is a journalist, editor and author who lives in London. She is the co-author, with Caroline Craig, of The Little Book of Lunch, and a columnist for Guardian Cook.

10 9 8 7 6 5 4 3 2 1

Square Peg, an imprint of Vintage,
20 Vauxhall Bridge Road,
London SW1V 2SA

Square Peg is part of the Penguin Random House group of companies
whose addresses can be found at global.penguinrandomhouse.com

◨ SQUARE PEG

www.vintage-books.co.uk

A CIP catalogue record for this book is available from the British Library

ISBN 9780224101042

Printed and bound in China by C&C Offset Printing Co. Ltd.
Art Direction: Charlotte Heal
Design: Kat Jenkins at Charlotte Heal Design
Photography by Charlotte Bland
www.charlottebland.co.uk
Food styling and home economy by Sophie Missing and Caroline Craig